The iPad

FOR PHOTOGRAPHERS

SECOND EDITION

Master the Newest Tool in Your Camera Bag

JEFF CARLSON

PEACHPIT PRESS

The iPad for Photographers:
Master the Newest Tool in Your Camera Bag, Second edition
Jeff Carlson

Peachpit Press
www.peachpit.com

To report errors, please send a note to errata@peachpit.com
Peachpit Press is a division of Pearson Education

Project Editor: Susan Rimerman
Production Editor: Tracey Croom
Copyeditor/Proofreader: Scout Festa
Indexer: Karin Arrigoni
Composition: Jeff Carlson
Cover Design/Photo Collage: Mimi Heft
Interior Design: Mimi Heft

ISBN 13: 978-0-321-90747-9
ISBN 10: 0-321-90747-7

9 8 7 6 5 4 3 2 1
Printed and bound in the United States of America

For Steve. Thank you.

Acknowledgments

It's fabulous to experience a whisper of an idea turn into a completed book, but without the encouragement and assistance of many people, that whisper could have easily dissipated into the ether. I owe a lot of gratitude, and no doubt coffees or martinis (or both) to the following good folks.

Susan Rimerman, Ted Waitt, Cliff Colby, Nancy Aldrich-Ruenzel, Nancy Davis, Scott Cowlin, Sara Jane Todd, and everyone else at Peachpit Press encouraged this project and made it happen.

Mimi Heft designed the book and provided first-class templates in which I could work. Unlike many authors, I write directly into the book's layout using Adobe InDesign, so working in a template that's properly styled and professionally designed is a privilege.

My editing and production team, led by Susan Rimerman, made all the practicalities happen: Scout Festa made me wish I could write as fast and as sharp as she's able to copyedit my text; Karin Arrigoni managed the crush at the end of the project to produce a top-rate index; and Tracey Croom put her production talents to good use shepherding the laid-out files and keeping my work on the up-and-up.

Chris Morse and Chris Horne gave me access to pre-release versions of their app Photosmith, and Brian Gerfort helped me understand better the underpinnings of how iOS works with images.

Glenn Fleishman helped maintain my link to the outside world as virtual officemate—and occasional in-person lunch or coffee companion—and patiently listened to my laments and successes.

Agen G. N. Schmitz also put up with my electronic chatter, but more importantly wrote the online chapter "Helpful Apps for Photographers."

Dana and David Bos granted permission for me to use photos I've shot of their daughter, Ainsley.

Jackie Baisa contributed advice and insight into professional workflows.

Peter Loh provided invaluable photo studio equipment.

Tor Bjorklund donated the wood used in many of the studio photos.

Kim Carlson built the App Reference appendix and served as a fantastic photographer's assistant and propmaster, but most importantly kept me sane and supported this project from my first inkling of an idea.

And Ellie Carlson continues to serve as a great model and a good sport when I turn the camera on her. She'll thank me when she's older. Right?

Contents

Introduction

Photographers carry gear. It doesn't matter whether you're a pro with multiple camera bodies and lenses or a casual shooter with an ever-present point-and-shoot camera—there's always stuff to pack along. And if you're traveling or away from your office or studio, part of that gear typically includes a laptop for reviewing and backing up the photos you take. Too often I've heard friends who are about to go on vacation moan that they need to bring a bulky computer just to handle their digital photos.

The iPad is changing all that.

Measuring less than half an inch thick and weighing about 1.3 pounds, the iPad is a fantastic device to take into the field. With the addition of an inexpensive iPad camera adapter, you can import photos directly from a camera or memory card and view them on the iPad's large color screen, revealing details that the relatively puny LCD on the back of your camera may obscure. More important, a rich array of photography apps and related products is adding to the list of things the iPad can do with those photos: rate and add keywords, perform color adjustments, retouch blemishes, and share the results online.

Oh, and don't forget all of the iPad's other capabilities: browsing the Web, accessing your email, reading ebooks, playing movies and music, and, as they say, so much more.

Can You Really Leave the Laptop Behind?

Although the iPad can do a lot that you would have needed a laptop to do just two years ago, there are still some important limitations that you should keep in mind when you decide whether a laptop stays at home.

If you're generating a significant amount of image data, storage becomes a problem. As this book goes to press, the current highest-capacity iPad holds 128 GB. You can free up some memory by removing apps, music, videos, and the like, but if you're filling multiple 16 GB or 32 GB cards with photos, the iPad won't work as a repository of your shots. (But I detail several workarounds in Chapter 2.)

One solution is to buy a lot of memory cards and use them as you would film canisters. The originals stay on the cards, while the keepers remain on the iPad; you delete the ones you don't want as you cull through them. Fortunately, memory cards are inexpensive now. *Un*fortunately, they're small and easy to lose. Make sure you know where they are, label them accurately, and keep them protected. Most important, make sure you have some system of backing up your images; options include uploading them to online photo storage services or transferring them wirelessly to a Wi-Fi–enabled hard disk like the Seagate Wireless Plus.

If you capture raw-formatted images, you won't benefit from the same level of editing that a dedicated application on a desktop computer can offer. With a few exceptions, all image editing occurs on JPEG versions of the raw files, and exports as JPEG files (see Chapter 5 for more details).

So, to answer my question, in many circumstances yes, you can leave the laptop behind. If you're going to trek across Africa for four weeks, that's likely not realistic, but for most day trips or short vacations, the iPad makes a great companion.

Which iPad Should You Use?

If you don't already own an iPad, here are some guidelines for choosing one that will be a worthwhile addition to your camera bag.

For the reasons mentioned, I recommend getting the highest-capacity iPad that's available (and that you can afford). That gives you plenty of room to store photos and apps; some image editors make a copy of a photo to work with, so you could easily fill a couple of gigabytes just editing. Plus, it's an iPad, not just an extra hard disk, so you'll want to store music, movies, books, and all sorts of other media.

Size and weight are also extremely important factors. Until last year, you bought whatever iPad was available, because they were all mostly the same. But then Apple introduced the svelte and light iPad mini, which is really a great traveling size. The tradeoff is that the iPad mini's screen measures 7.9 inches (versus 9.7 inches for the regular iPad) and doesn't have a high-resolution Retina display like its older sibling. Even so, the size is definitely compelling, and it's fine for reviewing and editing images. (If Apple releases an iPad mini with a Retina screen, that's likely to be my choice for my next iPad.)

You also need to determine whether you want to buy a model that connects to the Internet via Wi-Fi only or that also connects via cellular networking. For photographic uses, cellular isn't as important, because you may burn up your data allotment quickly if you transfer images to sharing sites or to online backup sources like Dropbox. (And it's turning out that even when a cellular provider offers "unlimited" data plans, they're not really unlimited.) I personally find the cellular capability useful in general iPad use, but not necessarily for photo-related uses.

In terms of which iPad model to get if you don't own one yet, I'd argue for the latest model. As I write this, Apple sells the fourth-generation iPad with Retina display, the iPad mini, and the iPad 2 as the line's low-cost point of entry. The iPad 2 is a fine model for photographers (it's what I used to write the first edition of this book), but your investment will last longer if you buy a newer model. The original iPad will also work in many cases, but just barely—its older processor and small amount of working memory prevent it from running iOS 6, and many developers (at Apple's insistence) are starting to phase out support for older versions of the operating system.

What's New in the Second Edition

As more photographers and developers have adopted the iPad, more and better uses for it as a photo companion continue to appear. This second edition of the book includes a host of new or changed material. Here are some highlights.

The cameras in the iPad 2 were so bad that I didn't want to touch this topic, but improvements in hardware convinced me that it was time to talk about taking photos with the iPad. Chapter 1 looks at the built-in Camera app as well as a few alternatives.

When I wrote the first edition, the only option for transferring photos wirelessly from the camera to the iPad was via an Eye-Fi memory card. Chapter 2 now includes mention of more wireless SD cards and adapters, including the CamRanger and CameraMator devices. More important, I shifted my recommendation away from Eye-Fi's software to the superior ShutterSnitch app, which supports most of the new devices. Chapter 2 also beefs up the section on making backups and adds that topic to the workflow diagrams.

Speaking of wireless communications, OnOne discontinued their DSLR Camera Remote app, which occupied the bulk of Chapter 3. Instead, I go into detail about using the CamRanger and CameraMator to shoot tethered—without wires this time—and control the camera remotely. Also new is a section on TriggerTrap, which adds all sorts of novel ways to control how a DSLR's shutter is fired.

When I first wrote Chapter 4, I was using a pre-release version of Photosmith because it was the only app that could import, rate, and tag photos on the iPad. The reality of publishing deadlines meant that some of the information quickly became outdated when Photosmith 2 shipped. For example, I talked about using the Seagate GoFlex Satellite drive to make wireless backups of photos from the app; however, a bug in the GoFlex firmware cropped up that corrupted data transfers (and Seagate never bothered to address it), so the feature was pulled from the app. This time around, I was able to again work with a pre-release version, but in this case it is for the revamped Photosmith 3 (which addresses the stability issues of version 2). My thanks go out again to developers Chris Morse and Chris Horne for trusting me enough to put their pre-release baby into my book.

Chapter 4 also had its own surprise: Pixelsync, the app I included that was used to sync photos with Aperture, is also discontinued. (The developer is working on a new app called Pixelstream, but timing prevented me from including it in this edition.) In Pixelsync's place, I've included details about PhotosInfoPro, a streamlined way of rating and tagging that exports sidecar files for importing into any photo management application that supports XMP files.

Chapter 5 incorporates sections about Apple's iPhoto app and Adobe's Photoshop Touch app that I wrote shortly after the first edition appeared—literally, the book was on press when Apple announced the third-generation iPad and iPhoto—and which was available as a downloadable addendum.

Last of the major changes, I had to pull the chapter "Helpful Apps for Photographers" from the print version of this edition due to page count restrictions. Look for a link to it online at ipadforphotographers.com. If you purchased an ebook this bonus appendix is already included.

There are lots of little changes here and there that aren't worth calling out specifically, so in short I'll say: I'm proud that this is a meaty update to the first edition.

Notes About This Book

As you read, you'll run into examples where I've adopted general terms or phrases to avoid getting distracted by details. For example, I frequently refer to the "computer" or the "desktop" as shorthand for any traditional computer that isn't the iPad. Although the iPad is most certainly a computer, I'm making the distinction between it and other computing devices, such as laptops, towers, all-in-one machines, and other hardware that runs OS X or Windows. When those details are important to a task, I note specific applications or computers.

The same general rule applies to iPad models. The iPad mini, despite its size, is still a fully functional iPad, so when I refer to "iPad" in general it applies to the iPad mini as well as the larger flagship model.

I also assume you're familiar with the way an iPad works—using gestures such as taps and swipes, syncing with a computer, connecting to the Internet, charging the battery, and otherwise taking care of your tablet. If you're brand new to the iPad, allow me a shameless plug as I encourage you to buy my *iPad Pocket Guide* (also from Peachpit Press).

Don't be surprised when you frequently run across the phrase, "As I write this." Both the iPad and the software useful to photographers are advancing rapidly, which makes this an exciting topic to cover.

Throughout the book, you'll find QR codes in the margins that provide shortcuts to the software or Web site mentioned. Download a free app such as QR Reader for iPad and scan the code to jump directly to the iTunes Store (in the case of an app) or Web site (A, on the next page); the code at right takes you to the product page for QR Reader.

QR Reader

A Using QR Reader to scan a QR code that leads to the QR Reader app in the iTunes Store. I think I just broke the universe.

If you don't want to deal with QR codes, or you're reading this on the very same iPad that you'd use to scan a QR code, you'll find URLs in the App Reference appendix at the end of the book.

To stay abreast of the changing field, be sure to visit the companion site for this book, www.ipadforphotographers.com, where I'll post updates and information related to the newest tool in your camera bag.

I've also set up an iPad for Photographers community on Google+ (which has turned into a popular social destination for photographers) for readers and others to share photos and conversation. (Here's the URL if you haven't yet downloaded a QR reader: https://plus.google.com/communities/111822708330207901957)

iPad for
Photographers
Web site

iPad for
Photographers
Google+
Community

Have fun shooting, and please feel free to contact me at the sites above with feedback!

CHAPTER 1

Capture Photos with the iPad

The iPad 2 was the first iPad to include cameras—one front-facing for FaceTime videoconferencing and one rear-facing—and boy were they terrible. The hardware was clearly added just to take advantage of FaceTime and because Apple's other iOS devices had cameras, not because Apple wanted to make the iPad a great photo-capture device.

In the first edition of this book, I recommended that readers ignore the photo capabilities. The results were just too painful. However, as the iPad's cameras have improved in the third and fourth generations and the iPad mini, I now regularly see people shooting photos or videos with their iPads. Although the form factor is awkward, I understand the appeal: Framing shots is easier when you have a large virtual viewfinder. The iPad mini seems like a better device for capturing photos, if only because it's not guaranteed to obscure the view of a person standing behind you.

Mostly, though, I think people shoot with an iPad because it's there. As the saying goes, "the best camera is the one you have with you." The built-in Camera app will get the job done, but I also want to highlight a few apps that will give you better results.

Shoot with the Camera App

When you're looking for something that quickly captures a shot, the iPad's Camera app gets the job done. It takes photos and saves them to the Camera Roll, where you can view, edit, or share them (see Chapter 5 for details). Although it is roughly the same app as on the iPhone, Camera on the iPad doesn't have the same features—you won't find a flash (there's no hardware for it) or the ability to make HDR or panorama images. Still, it's simple—which is the whole point.

1. Open the Camera app.

2. To toggle between the rear and front cameras, tap the Camera Switch button.

3. Frame your shot on the screen, in either landscape or portrait orientation.

4. The iPad attempts to focus on whatever is in the center of the frame. If you see one or more green boxes appear, the app is identifying what it thinks is a person's face and using that as the focus point. You can focus on any other area by tapping once on the item on the screen (1.1).

   Tapping once also sets the overall exposure for the image. If you'd like to lock the focus and exposure, touch and hold an area for 2–3 seconds. You'll see an "AE/AF Lock" indicator at the bottom of the screen. Tapping anywhere removes the lock.

5. To help you line up the photo, tap the Options button and enable the onscreen grid.

6. To capture a photo, tap the shutter button at the right edge of the screen.

   ▶ **TIP** Tapping the shutter button can subtly move the iPad itself, resulting in pictures that may be slightly blurry due to camera shake. To get around this, touch and hold the button, frame your shot, and then lift your finger.

Shooting a video follows the same approach: Tap the Photo/Video switch to Video and tap the Record button to start capturing footage; tap it again to stop recording.

Shoot with Advanced Apps

As a photographer, you expect more control over how you capture images. Apple has made the iPad's camera a simple point-and-shoot operation, but the hardware is far more capable. That's where outside developers come in.

You'll find dozens of apps that go beyond basic picture-taking, from novelty apps that apply image filters to more complicated ones that fill in the gaps that Apple has left open. I couldn't hope to cover them all here—it would take away your fun of exploring, and selections are always changing. So instead, I'm going to focus on a few I've used that offer advanced features like separate focus and exposure control, timed shooting modes, and HDR (high dynamic range) imaging.

Set Focus and Exposure

It's convenient to set the focus and exposure based on a single area of a photo, but the two attributes aren't always tied together. The camera will try to achieve a perfectly exposed image overall, which can lead to, for example, subjects in the foreground appearing dark in order to prevent a bright background from blowing out to white. But sometimes you may want that—getting a well-lit shot of someone may be more important than having a properly balanced background.

**Camera+
for iPad**

Camera+ for iPad initially uses a single selector. Tap once to establish a focus point and then tap the attached (+) button to reveal separate Focus and Exposure selectors (1.2). Drag each one to set the focus point and exposure setting. (Focus is the primary control, so you can tap anywhere to redefine which area is sharp; you must drag the Exposure control.) Reframing the iPad will cause those settings to change, so if you want to lock one of them, tap the Lock button in the lower-left corner of the screen and choose which variable to lock.

1.2 Splitting the Focus and Exposure selectors in Camera+

> ▶ **TIP** Many cameras and lenses offer image stabilization to minimize the effect of camera shake while you're shooting. Camera+ includes a Stabilizer mode that doesn't take the shot until the iPad has stopped moving. Tap the Mode button (the gear above the shutter button) and choose Stabilizer. If the iPad is moving too much, the shutter button turns red to remind you to stop moving; the app won't capture the shot until the iPad is relatively stable.

Time Your Shots

Some situations call for different shot timing than just one person pressing the shutter button. In Camera+, tap the Mode button above the shutter button to choose a mode:

- **Timer.** Selecting this option switches to a 5-second timer that counts down after you tap the shutter button. You can change the duration by tapping the Set Timer indicator in the middle of the screen—5, 15, or 30 seconds.

- **Burst.** When this feature is active, holding the shutter button down fires off multiple shots. The iPad doesn't need to shuttle images to a memory card, so unlike with most cameras you won't run into a lag as the images buffer to memory; I accidentally grabbed about 75 photos over a few seconds without realizing it. Burst mode comes at a cost, however: To achieve this performance, images are captured at a measly 640 by 480 pixels.

Blux Camera for iPad

Filters and Editing in Camera Apps

Many camera apps don't stop at capturing images. They want you to stick with them from shot to share, so you'll find a bevy of editing features included. Choose image filters that simulate analog cameras or colored filters, apply textures and borders, and adjust aspects such as exposure and white balance. If you like to experiment with looks as you're shooting, try Blux Camera for iPad, which applies effects to the live image before you capture the shot (**1.3**). I cover dedicated editing apps in Chapter 5.

1.3 Preview effects in Blux Camera for iPad.

Shoot HDR Photos

HDR (high dynamic range) is a technique for solving a common problem in photography: getting enough exposure in all areas of a scene without sections being plunged into darkness or blown out to white. HDR software combines two or more exposures—typically a dark one and a light one—into one balanced image. The iPhone includes HDR as a shooting mode, but the iPad doesn't, leaving us to turn to outside software.

TrueHDR

I like the TrueHDR app, which offers three capture modes as well as the ability to process photos you've already shot or imported. The Auto mode evaluates the scene and determines light and dark exposures for capturing two shots. The SemiAuto and Manual modes give you the opportunity to define your own light and dark areas. After merging the shots, you can adjust warmth, saturation, contrast, and brightness to tailor the result (1.4).

1.4 Fine-tuning a TrueHDR image

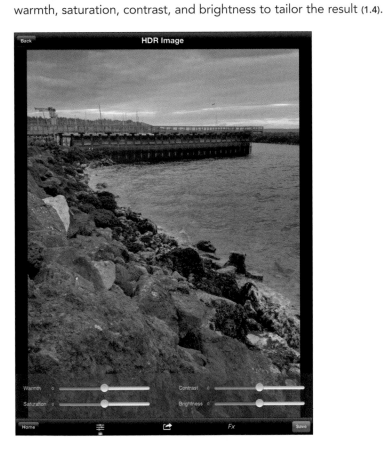

Create a Panorama

A snapshot is a specific slice of space and time, framed by the bounds of the camera's lens. But you can break out of that frame—or at least push its borders—by capturing a panorama. The iPad takes multiple photos as you pan across a scene, and then stitches them together to create one long image. (And yep, you guessed it: The Camera app on the iPhone includes a great panorama feature that isn't included on the iPad.)

AutoStitch
Panorama
for iPad

You'll find plenty of panorama apps at the App Store, including AutoStitch Panorama for iPad. AutoStitch employs the iPad's accelerometer to help line up images as you shoot and offers a colored indicator to signal when areas overlap well (green) or poorly (yellow or red) (1.5). After capturing the shots, the app stitches them together and gives you the option to crop the result into a clean rectangular photo.

1.5 Overlap images to capture a good panorama.

CHAPTER 2

The iPad on Location

Through the years, I've hauled various laptops on vacations and business trips, and although the computers have gotten smaller and lighter over time, carrying one and its assorted peripherals still takes up a lot of space and weight. In contrast, the slim size and weight of the iPad (especially the iPad mini) makes it an ideal traveling companion. As a photographer, you probably already carry a fair amount of gear. Wouldn't you like to lighten your bag further?

Instead of squinting at the LCD panel on the back of the camera, view your shots on the iPad's brilliant 9.7-inch or 7.9-inch screen and pick out details in the middle of a shoot that you may miss through the viewfinder. You can also use the iPad as a remote photo studio. Sort, rate, and apply metadata to the images while you're traveling, or edit and share them to your favorite social networks. And then, when you're back at home or in your studio, bring the photos into your computer, ready for further editing in Lightroom or other software. Whether "on location" is somewhere truly remote or just your back yard, the iPad can be your new photographer's assistant.

Build an iPad Photo Workflow

Before stepping outside with your camera, it's important to figure out how you want to capture images that will end up on the iPad. The question of whether to shoot images in raw format or JPEG format initially seems irrelevant to the iPad—the device can import both types. But choosing one (or both) leads to considerations that ripple through the entire iPad workflow. So let's take the time to look at this first. (The table below provides a quick overview of the discussion.)

Raw image files contain the unaltered information captured by the camera's image sensor, which provides much more data to work with when editing in a desktop program such as Adobe Photoshop, Adobe Photoshop Lightroom, or Apple's Aperture. In general, professional and intermediate cameras offer a raw capture option.

JPEG files, on the other hand, are processed within the camera before they're saved. Each image is color corrected, sharpened, compressed, and adjusted in other ways to create what the camera believes is the best image.

When brought into an image editor on the desktop, a JPEG file doesn't offer as much image data and therefore can't be edited as thoroughly as a raw file. For example, you're more likely to successfully pull detail out of shadow areas with a raw file than with a JPEG. All digital cameras can capture JPEG images; for some models, JPEG is the only choice.

Read on for an overview of the options. Although I assume you want to shoot raw if you're able to—after all, the ultimate consideration is usually image quality—some situations may call for you to switch formats.

	Import to iPad	Rate & Tag Images	Edit Images	Sync to Computer
JPEG	Fast	Yes	Yes, but limited image information is available. Quality starts out compressed. Edited versions are saved as copies.	Easy import into desktop software or folder
Raw	Slower	Yes	Not directly in most apps. Edits apply to the JPEG preview. Lose the full advantage of editing raw files.	Raw files are imported into desktop software; any edited versions (JPEGs) are imported separately.
Raw+ JPEG	Slowest; uses the most disk space	Yes; treated as one image	JPEG portion is edited, while raw remains untouched. JPEG is often better quality than auto-generated preview.	Bring raw files and edited JPEGs into desktop software; delete other JPEGs (depending on software).

Shoot JPEG

If your camera doesn't shoot in raw format, JPEG is your only option. You might also choose to capture JPEGs when you're deliberately shooting snapshots that need to be processed or shared quickly, or when you want to employ the simplest workflow (2.1).

1. Capture photos in JPEG format on your camera.

2. Import the photos into the iPad (discussed in detail later in this chapter).

3. Back up your images (also explained later in the chapter).

4. Review the photos using the Photos app.

5. Optionally edit, rate, tag, or share pictures.

6. Synchronize the pictures to photo software on your computer when you're back at home or the office.

2.1 Workflow for shooting in JPEG format

Capture JPEG

Import into iPad   Back up

Edit   Rate/tag   Share

Export to computer

The main advantage of the JPEG workflow is that it's largely friction free. Photos occupy less storage space on the iPad, making even the lowest-capacity model workable for holding pictures on location. You also deal with just one set of images, unlike with raw files (as you'll see shortly).

The primary disadvantage is that JPEG images are compressed and corrected within the camera, so you're not getting the fullest possible image data. Editing images, whether on the iPad or on the desktop, further reduces image quality, because the JPEG format applies *lossy* compression—image data is removed from the file whenever it's saved. If you edit the images on the iPad, many editing apps apply still more compression. When you bring the photos into the computer, you don't have as much latitude for editing them.

I don't mean to sound alarmist, as if shooting in JPEG is going to produce muddled images. JPEG compression is based on how the eye perceives images and is generally very good. It's just that, when compared to working with a raw file, JPEG files start you at a disadvantage.

Shoot Raw

Capturing photos in raw format adds some complexity to the iPad workflow (2.2). Although the iPad can import raw files, it can't edit them natively (in most cases; see Chapter 5 to learn about apps that *are* able to manipulate raw files directly). Instead, any editing or sharing is done on JPEG previews supplied by the camera.

1. Capture photos in raw format on your camera.

2. Import the pictures into the iPad.

3. Back up your images.

4. If you edit or share photos on the iPad, the work is done on the JPEG previews. Edited versions are saved as new JPEG files, and the raw files remain untouched.

5. If you rate and tag photos on the iPad, the metadata is retained when photos are exported from the iPad to the photo software on your computer (see Chapter 4).

6. Since any images you edited on the iPad are separate versions, they're added to your photo software. For images you didn't edit, the JPEG previews are ignored.

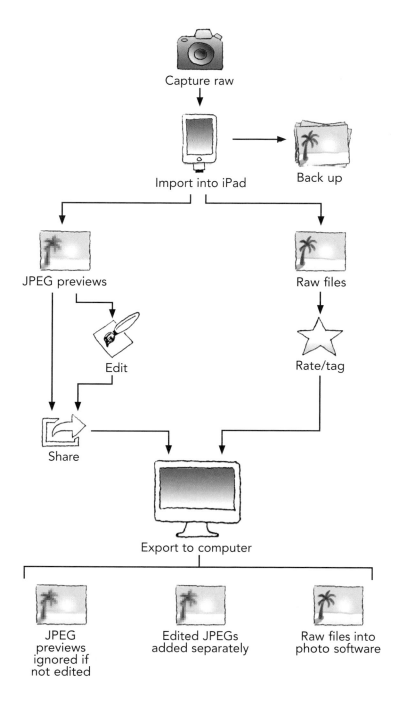

Capture raw

Import into iPad

Back up

JPEG previews

Raw files

Edit

Rate/tag

Share

Export to computer

JPEG previews ignored if not edited

Edited JPEGs added separately

Raw files into photo software

► **TIP** One option is to consider editing on the iPad a temporary step: Edit images to share them quickly when you know you won't be back at the computer for a while, and then dump those edited versions when syncing to the computer, where you can edit the originals with better tools.

The advantage to the raw workflow is that you retain all of the image data for later editing, giving you the most flexibility with the photos on the desktop. Also, metadata that you add stays with the raw images, so you don't need to undertake another round of rating and keyword tagging on the computer.

However, a main disadvantage is that raw files occupy much more storage space, which is an issue if you're shooting hundreds or thousands of photos. Most editing apps work only on JPEG previews, so you can't take full advantage of the raw image data unless you use a dedicated raw editing app. Also, unless the iPad is acting as just temporary storage between camera and computer, you end up with separate JPEG versions that must also be imported (unless you dump the JPEG versions).

Shoot Raw+JPEG

For cameras that support it, a third option is to shoot in Raw+JPEG mode. In this case, the camera writes two files: the raw file, plus a JPEG file as specified by the camera settings instead of an automatically generated preview file. The workflow looks something like this **(2.3)**:

1. Shoot photos using the camera's Raw+JPEG mode.

2. Import the photos into the iPad, which displays just one thumbnail for each image and a "RAW+JPG" badge, although each image is made up of a raw file and a JPEG file.

3. Back up the images.

4. Optionally edit and/or share photos, which applies to the JPEG counterpart for each photo. Edited images are saved as new JPEG files.

5. Rate and tag images. The Raw+JPEG pair is treated as a single image.

6. Export the photos to your computer. The Raw+JPEG pair is treated as one image, although you can choose to work on the versions separately; Aperture, for example, gives you the option to import just the raw file, to import just the JPEG, or to import both files and specify which is the "master" for the pair.

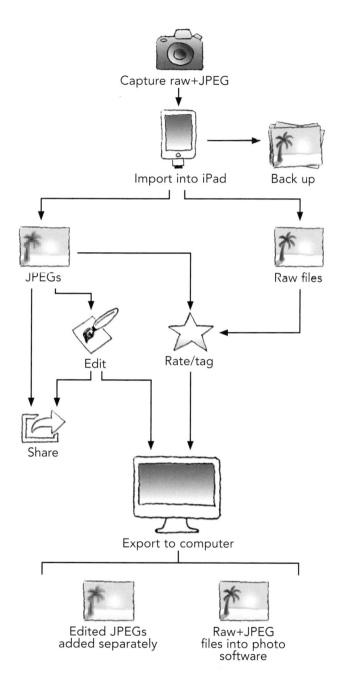

Capture raw+JPEG

Import into iPad

Back up

JPEGs

Raw files

Edit

Rate/tag

Share

Export to computer

Edited JPEGs
added separately

Raw+JPEG
files into photo
software

2.3 Shooting
Raw+JPEG using
one memory card

On some high-end cameras that accept two simultaneous memory cards, you can specify that raw files be written to one card and JPEG files to the other. This implementation can be somewhat cleaner, treating the raw files as "digital negatives" that exist separately from the iPad (2.4):

1. Capture photos in Raw+JPEG format, specifying that raw files are written to one card and JPEG files are written to the other.

2. Import the JPEG images into the iPad. Leave the raw files on the card and store it in your camera bag.

3. Back up your images. That's not as easy in this workflow as in the others, because the raw files aren't on the iPad. You can get away with using the card as the backup, of course. If you were to lose the card, you'd still have the JPEGs on the iPad. But if you're paranoid (and there's a good case for paranoia—these are your original images, after all), you'll need a backup device that can copy the image files directly from the card. See "Back Up Your Photos," later in this chapter.

4. Edit and/or share the JPEG files on the iPad.

5. Rate and tag images. Although you're applying metadata to the JPEGs, it's possible to transfer the data to the raw files on your computer via Photosmith's Lightroom sync feature or by exporting XML sidecar files created in PhotosInfoPro. (See Chapter 4 for details.)

6. Export edited versions of the JPEGs to the computer; delete the rest.

7. Export the raw files to your computer.

The primary advantage of shooting Raw+JPEG is that you have more control over the JPEG files that you import into the iPad. If your intent is to quickly preview and share photos from the iPad with a little editing here and there, and if you can save to separate cards, you can specify a smaller JPEG image size in your camera's settings. That speeds up import time and saves storage space on the iPad without affecting image quality much. Also, the raw originals are still available for editing on your computer.

The disadvantage is that Raw+JPEG when saved to a single card takes up more storage space. Recording to two cards helps in terms of storage but complicates the process in terms of backing up original raw files and syncing metadata in the computer.

I often shoot just raw images and bring them into the iPad. When I know I'll be editing on the iPad, I'll shoot Raw+JPEG to take advantage of the higher-resolution images. If I owned a camera capable of recording to dual memory cards, however, I'd probably shoot Raw+JPEG and split the versions between them. That works particularly well when transferring files wirelessly; raw files write to a regular SD card, and JPEGs write to the Wi-Fi card to take advantage of the faster transfer speed afforded by the smaller file sizes.

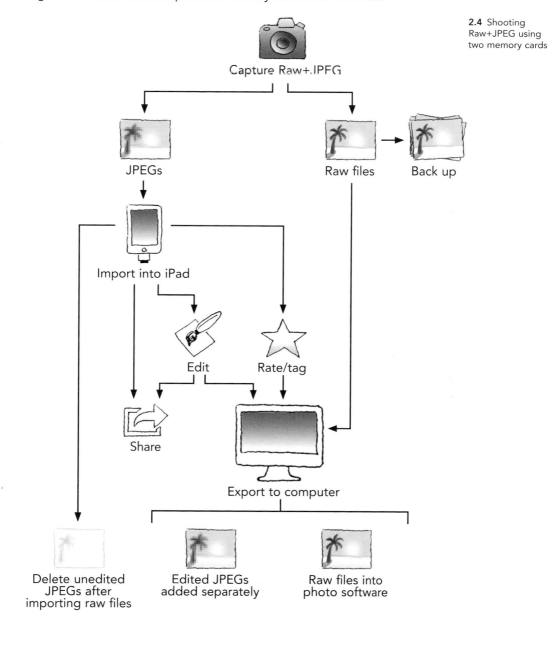

2.4 Shooting Raw+JPEG using two memory cards

Review Photos in the Field

The shift from film to digital cameras brought an enhancement that fundamentally changed the way photographers shoot. It's second nature for us now, but the ability to take a shot and review it on the camera's LCD for feedback was a real revolution. You could tell right away if you needed to adjust the exposure, you could check whether everyone in the shot was looking at the camera, and you could otherwise see what was just recorded to the memory card.

And yet. Camera screens have improved over the years, in both resolution and size, but it's not always easy to spot details on a 3-inch screen. The iPad's 9.7-inch screen—and even the iPad mini's 7.9-inch screen—reveals plenty of detail, without involving the bulk and inconvenience of a laptop.

Using an inexpensive adapter from Apple, you can import shots from a memory card or from a camera directly and get a better view of your photos—while you're shooting on location, not later at home when the shot is no longer available. It's also possible to transfer photos to the iPad wirelessly using Wi-Fi–equipped memory cards or add-on devices.

In this section, I'm making the assumption that you've left the computer at home and have the iPad on location—whether far-flung or just out and about for a couple of hours. There may be times when you want to review photos on the iPad even with a laptop available; I cover such situations in the next chapter, "The iPad in the Studio."

Import Using the iPad Camera Adapters

Apple's iPad camera adapters rank among the few truly essential iPad accessories; without them, I wouldn't have been able to write this book! If you own a third-generation or earlier iPad (with a 30-pin dock), you want the $29 iPad Camera Connection Kit. It's made up of two pieces that attach to the iPad's dock connector: an adapter that accepts SD memory cards, and one that accepts a standard USB plug. If you own an iPad mini or fourth-generation or later iPad, you can buy the Lightning to SD Card Camera Reader or the Lightning to USB Camera Adapter, sold separately for $29 each (2.5). Or, if you already own the 30-pin adapters and have upgraded to a Lightning-equipped iPad, you can get away with the Lightning to 30-pin Adapter, which also costs $29.

2.5 Camera adapters are available for whichever iPad you own.

Import from a memory card or camera

When you're ready to transfer the photos you shot, do the following:

1. Remove the SD card from your camera and insert it into the SD card adapter. Or, connect the USB cable that came with the camera (typically a USB-to-mini-USB cable) between the USB adapter and the camera's USB port.

2. Wake the iPad if it's not already on.

3. Insert the adapter into the iPad's dock connector. If you're connecting via USB, you may also need to power on the camera or switch it into its review or playback mode. The Photos app automatically launches and displays thumbnails of the memory card's contents (2.6, next page).

When importing Raw+JPEG images, the format is marked on their thumbnails (2.7). You can't choose whether to import JPEG or raw independently, though.

4. If you wish to bring in all of the photos, tap the Import All button. Otherwise, tap the thumbnails of just the photos you want; a blue checkmark icon indicates a photo is selected. Unfortunately, there's no option to view a larger version of the shots at this point. There's also no easy way to select a range of thumbnails other than tapping each one. (iOS 4 actually included a great shortcut: touch and hold one photo, and then drag to select others without lifting your finger. That capability disappeared in iOS 5; I'm hoping the shortcut returns in a future software update.)

5. Tap the Import button (2.8). You still have the opportunity to ignore your selections and import everything by tapping the Import All button. Or, tap Import Selected to copy the ones you chose in the last step. The photos begin copying to the iPad's memory; a green checkmark icon tells you the photo has been imported.

2.7 Raw+JPEG files are clearly identified.

2.8 Import only the photos you want.

▶ **TIP** It can take a while to import a full memory card, but you don't have to put the iPad down. Photos continue to copy in the background, even if you switch to another app.

6. After the photos are copied, you're asked if you want to delete the imported files from the memory card. I recommend tapping the Keep button and then erasing the card using the camera's controls.

   The images appear in your Photo Library in two new, automatically created albums: Last Import and All Imported.

7. At this point, you can remove the adapter—no need to eject it, as you would on a computer. The Photos app switches to the Last Import album, where you can review the imported photos.

When the Photos app scans an inserted memory card, it identifies shots you've already imported with a green checkmark. For example, suppose you're shooting with the same card that you used yesterday because there's still plenty of free space left on it. If you tap the Import All button, you're asked if you want to re-import all of the photos—in which case you end up with multiple copies—or to skip the duplicates.

▶ **TIP** As you can see from the screenshots, the import process also gives you the option of deleting images from the memory card. This feature is great if you want to keep using a card for shooting but don't want to save obviously poor photos. For example, I don't need to retain dozens of test and setup shots while I'm trying to dial in the right settings and lighting positions. Tap to select the photos you wish to remove, and then tap the Delete button.

What About Importing from CompactFlash (CF) Cards?

You can connect the USB adapter to your camera, but of course that ties up your camera while the photos are downloading. Instead, plug the card into a CompactFlash USB reader and connect that via the USB adapter. However, there's a catch: It doesn't work with all readers. The iPad imposes a limit of 20 mA to the amount of power an accessory can draw. If the card reader requires more, it won't work (unless the reader is connected to a powered hub, and the hub is connected to the iPad; but a powered hub won't help you if you're on location without an electricity source). I can't recommend any particular models, since the market changes frequently, but a search for CompactFlash adapters for iPad will reveal models that other photographers have used successfully.

Import from an iPhone

While I was having coffee with a friend, he asked, "So, are you going to get the cool new camera?" I must have looked puzzled, because he followed up with a grin and, "You know, the camera that also has some smartphone features." He meant the iPhone 4S, which was then about to be released. He was far less interested in the specifications or new features of the device than in the substantial improvements made to its camera.

That camera is quite impressive, made more so by the fact that the iPhone is always with me. I can capture great shots without also carrying a separate camera all the time.

Getting photos from the iPhone into the iPad is as simple as importing from any other digital camera. Plug a regular iPhone sync cable into the iPad USB adapter, and then connect the iPhone and the iPad. Thumbnails appear in the Photos app, ready to be imported (2.9).

PhotoSync

Another direct import route from iPhone to iPad (or between any two iOS devices) is to transfer the photos wirelessly using an app called PhotoSync. As long as both devices are connected to the same Wi-Fi network, they can bounce images back and forth, like so:

1. On the iPad, launch PhotoSync and tap the red Sync button.

2. Tap the Receive Photos/Videos button.

2.9 Importing photos from an iPhone into the iPad

3. On the iPhone, launch PhotoSync and tap the thumbnail of the image or images you want to transfer.

4. Tap the Sync Selected button.

5. In the next dialog, tap the iPhone-iPod-iPad button to specify where you want to transfer the image or images to (2.10).

6. Tap the name of the iPad that appears. The photo or photos you selected copy from the iPhone to the iPad.

2.10 Transfer photos from an iPhone (shown) to an iPad using PhotoSync.

The Secretly Versatile iPad USB Camera Adapter

Skype

GarageBand

iMovie

The iPad USB camera adapters were designed to connect the iPad and digital cameras, but they work with other USB-based items, too. Need to type something lengthy but don't own a wireless keyboard? Plug in a USB one. Connect a wired USB headset and use the Skype app to talk to people via voice. Or, plug in a USB microphone, record to GarageBand or iMovie, and you have a portable podcasting studio (**2.11**).

There is one catch, though. As I mentioned in the "What About Importing from CompactFlash (CF) Cards?" sidebar, iOS imposes a 20 mA power limit on the USB connection. So, some accessories that draw more energy than that to function won't work. In that case, you need to connect the accessory to a powered USB hub. (One exception: I've seen some USB keyboards continue to function even after triggering the low-power alert.) Be sure to test any accessory before you go on location.

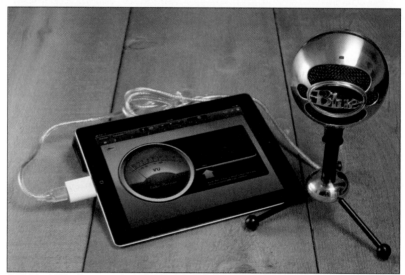

2.11 The USB adapter works with accessories such as this external microphone.

Import Wirelessly from the Camera

Wait a minute. We're in the second decade of the twenty-first century, viewing high-resolution digital photos on a tablet computer operated by touch. Do we need to shuttle files using adapters and cables as if we were using floppy disks? Isn't there another way, one that feels more like the future we live in?

How about taking a photo and having it appear on the iPad a few seconds later, using the camera you already own and without tethering it to the iPad via a cable? Using a wireless memory card or device, you can do exactly that. Eye-Fi, Toshiba, and Transcend each sell cards that look and work like regular SD memory cards, but also feature built-in radios that can connect to Wi-Fi networks or even create their own. Some cameras now include built-in Wi-Fi hardware or use manufacturer-specific adapters (like the Nikon WU-1b for some Nikon models). A handful of companies now also offer wireless devices that can control the camera from the iPad, such as the CamRanger and the CameraMator (see Chapter 3 for more information).

When shooting on location, you can't guarantee that a Wi-Fi network will be available. Each card and device is capable of creating its own wireless base station. After you connect the iPad to that wireless network, photos you shoot can be transferred shortly after they're captured.

As I write this, the SD cards are available in capacities of between 4 GB and 32 GB and range in price from $40 to $100. Be sure to check out the specifications for each device; the Eye-Fi Pro X2 model, for example, is the only Eye-Fi card that can import raw files.

> ► **TIP** Many cameras now include built-in support for Eye-Fi cards. The Nikon D600, for instance, recognizes when one is inserted and provides controls for enabling or disabling the wireless feature.

ShutterSnitch

Shoot and import wirelessly using ShutterSnitch

Each of these devices relies on its own iOS app for communicating with the iPad, but the implementation can be spotty. Instead, save yourself a headache and buy ShutterSnitch. (Make sure it supports your hardware first.)

I'm using Eye-Fi as the example, but the process is similar for other cards and wireless adapters. You'll first need to configure the card, using desktop software provided by the manufacturer to set up Direct Mode and any Wi-Fi networks it should recognize (like your home network). For these instructions, I'm assuming you're in the field, pith helmet and all, where Wi-Fi networks are scarce; if you're on a recognized home network, you can skip step 2.

1. Take a photo to activate the wireless card's Direct Mode. (It goes to sleep after a few minutes of inactivity to conserve power.)

2. On the iPad, go to Settings > Wi-Fi and select the Eye-Fi Card network (2.12).

3. Open ShutterSnitch and tap the New Collection (+) button.

4. Name the collection and tap Create, or just tap Create to use the current time as the name.

5. The test photo you just took automatically transfers to the iPad; any images on the card that had not yet been transferred are also copied.

6. Continue shooting. As you capture each shot, it's transferred to the iPad (2.13).

7. Tap a thumbnail to view the photo full-screen.

2.12 The Eye-Fi card shows up in the iPad's Wi-Fi settings.

2.13 Photos arrive in ShutterSnitch from the camera just after they're shot.

ShutterSnitch stores its photos within the app, so when you want to move them to your computer or make them accessible to editing apps, tap the Share button, select the images you want, and then choose an option from the Export button (the arrow pointing up); that can be the Camera Roll, Dropbox, email, or other apps.

ShutterSnitch as Photographer's Assistant

ShutterSnitch does more than just import photos. It displays pertinent metadata (ISO, aperture, shutter speed, and focal length) and can pop up warnings about that metadata that you specify. One of my annoying shooting traits is to forget to reset ISO, so too often I've started shooting at ISO 800 (or higher) even in well-lit situations. In ShutterSnitch, I created a warning that appears when any photo arrives with an ISO higher than 200 (**2.14**).

You can also set up action tasks to automate tasks within ShutterSnitch before exporting to another source. For example, you could rename a photo, add a watermark, and resize it for sharing.

2.14 ShutterSnitch warns that my ISO is high and highlights hot areas of the photo (in red).

> ► **TIP** Change the iPad's Auto-Lock setting to 15 minutes or Never when you're shooting with the Eye-Fi (go to Settings > General > Auto-Lock). If the iPad goes to sleep, it severs the connection to the Eye-Fi's network to conserve power. When you wake up the iPad, it may not automatically grab the network again (especially if you took a break in shooting, during which the Eye-Fi goes to sleep).

Shoot and import wirelessly using CameraMator

CameraMator

Devices like the CamRanger and CameraMator do more than just import photos wirelessly (as you'll see in Chapter 3), and because of that they use their own software for transferring images. I'm using CameraMator as the example here, but the others work in a similar fashion.

1. Turn on the device and connect to the wireless network it creates.

2. In the CameraMator software, tap Session Preview and choose your camera.

3. Take a photo using the camera. It appears in CameraMator and is also stored in the iPad's Camera Roll (2.15).

2.15 Reviewing a photo in CameraMator

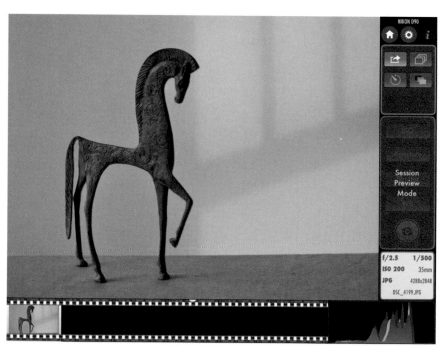

> ▶ **TIP** Normally, the CamRanger software reads only a thumbnail from the memory card to give you an idea of what you captured. Tap the Settings button, expand the Controls section, and enable the Auto View option to download full versions for review. However, the software doesn't actually store those photos on the iPad—you can view them full size while you're shooting, but if you exit the app and return later, the shots no longer appear. Tap the memory card button at the top left of the screen to view photos stored on the camera's memory card and download them to the iPad's Camera Roll.

CamRanger

Record Location Information

Have you ever looked at a photo and wondered where it was taken? Was it, unfortunately, one of your own photos? Thanks to the scientific marvel of GPS (Global Positioning System), you can add geolocation data to your photos and find their locations on a map.

Although GPS isn't a new technology, most cameras don't capture location data. A few cameras can be outfitted with GPS adapters that write the data directly to the photo files, and you can buy standalone GPS logging devices. However, you already own one: the iPad. Models that offer cellular networking include a GPS chip; Wi-Fi models can also perform some geolocation, but in a limited capacity because they need to know which Wi-Fi networks are nearby to determine location.

I'm going to highlight two iOS apps, both of which are designed for the iPhone but run fine on the iPad. Geotag Photos Pro records the data and then makes it available via the Web or Dropbox for you to import into a photo organizing application. GeoSnitch works with ShutterSnitch to apply the geolocation data to photos on the iPad itself.

Record Location Using Geotag Photos Pro

Geotag Photos Pro runs in the background on your iPad or iPhone, tracking your location. It then saves the data as a GPX (GPS eXchange format) file that can be read by many applications. I like it because the trip logs it creates can be automatically uploaded to my Dropbox folder, saving me the trouble of transferring the data to my computer later.

Geotag
Photos Pro

1. In Geotag Photos Pro, tap the New Trip button to name your recording session.

2. By default, the app logs your location every 2 minutes, but you can change that by tapping the Autolog button and specifying a time. The more frequently it records a location, the more battery it will consume.

▶ **TIP** Make sure the date and time listed matches the same information on your camera; it's possible to get the time back in sync after you shoot, but taking care of it now is easier. Tap the Settings button and then tap Setup Time on Camera.

3. Tap the Rec button to start recording (2.16).

4. When you're done shooting photos, open Geotag Photos Pro and tap the Stop button.

5. Tap the Trips History button, locate your trip, and tap the Share button.

6. Choose to share via email, iTunes, or Dropbox (2.17). (If you set up automatic Dropbox syncing, the GPX file will automatically appear on your computer.)

7. Import the photos into your computer, and use an application (such as Lightroom, or HoudahGeo on the Mac) to associate the geolocation data with the images.

2.16 Recording a trip

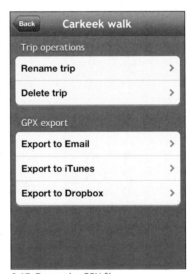

2.17 Export the GPX file.

Record Location Using GeoSnitch

When you launch GeoSnitch, the app identifies your current location and presents a prominent red button (2.18). Tap the red button to begin tracking.

GeoSnitch

▶ **TIP** ShutterSnitch can't associate GeoSnitch's data with raw files, so geo-tagging works only with JPEGs.

GeoSnitch samples the location every second—you don't need to do anything. You can put the iPad or iPhone to sleep and it will still save location data until you tap the red button again to stop.

After you finish shooting, import the photos into ShutterSnitch on the iPad and then do the following:

1. Open GeoSnitch and tap the List button.

2. Choose the recording that matches your photo session.

3. Tap the Open In button and choose ShutterSnitch. The app opens and matches the photos with the time stamps (2.19).

4. Tap the Tag Selected button to apply the geolocation data.

2.18 Track your location with GeoSnitch.

2.19 PhotoSnitch matches photos based on their time stamps.

Record Reference Photos Using the iPad

Having location capabilities built into the iPad (and iPhone) presents another geolocation option. Every photo you capture using the device automatically includes the location data. If you don't want to track every step or use third-party software, simply capture a shot using the iPad along with the photos you take with your camera. When you return to your computer, use desktop software to copy that GPS data and apply it to other shots taken at the same location. Aperture, for example, offers a nifty feature called Import GPS from iPhone Photos that applies the iPhone's data to photos you select.

"268 miles and
the 'revisit' tag"

Use GPS to Mark Locations to Revisit

My friend and photographer Rick LePage likes to get on his motorcycle and explore, and he often finds new potential photo spots. If he doesn't have the opportunity to capture some photos at the time (usually due to weather or timing), he takes a snapshot with his iPhone and then later adds a "revisit" tag to it. The embedded GPS data marks the location so he can head back when conditions are more favorable. Read more at www.135f2.com/2011/07/268-miles/.

Back Up Your Photos

The main focus of this chapter is to move photos from your camera to the iPad, but getting them off the tablet in the form of backups is just as important. When you're shooting in the field with your iPad in hand, you don't have the luxury of transferring dozens of gigabytes onto your computer or to an external hard drive attached to it. That leaves you with a few options.

You can import photos into the iPad and use the memory cards you shot with as backups. It's like carrying film rolls all over again—although in this scenario, they occupy much less physical space. Fortunately, the price of memory cards has steadily dropped as capacities have increased, so you're not spending a lot of money to pick up several 8 GB, 16 GB, or 32 GB cards.

If your iPad can connect to a speedy Wi-Fi Internet connection, you can upload images to a service such as Dropbox or to the Photo Stream feature of Apple's iCloud. I recognize that "speedy Wi-Fi Internet connection" can be a giant *if*. Maybe someday you'll be able to tap into a fast, high-capacity cellular network in a sheep pasture in Scotland, but chances are you'll be blissfully (or agonizingly) far from the rest of the world while you're shooting.

Or, after shooting for the day, you can return home or to a hotel room, or maybe park in a Wi-Fi–equipped coffee house for a few hours, and connect to a broadband Internet connection there (although even that possibility can be spotty, depending on location). But today's cellular networks are only starting to approach the speed and capacity required to upload dozens or hundreds of multi-megabyte files, and in most cases you pay a premium to do so.

It's not impossible, though. I've uploaded large files while sipping in a Starbucks, and I've dribbled files over a flaky 3G cellular connection next to a tent and campfire in the mountains.

What's important is to have some type of backup. Everything I discuss in this book becomes useless if you somehow lose the photos you went to such trouble to capture in the first place.

iCloud Photo Stream

I signed up for Apple's free iCloud service primarily to share my calendars and contacts between various devices, but I also got an added bonus: Photo Stream.

Whenever you take a photo using an iPhone, iPod touch, or iPad, it's saved to the device's Camera Roll. With Photo Stream enabled, each of those photos is automatically uploaded to iCloud and copied to your other enabled devices when they're connected to a Wi-Fi network. A photo captured by my iPhone, for example, shows up on my iPad, on my Apple TV at home, and on my MacBook Pro.

More importantly for our discussion here, any photos imported into the iPad using a camera adapter are added to the Camera Roll, so they, too, appear in your Photo Stream (2.20). (The same applies to screenshots you capture on an iOS device, which often makes my personal Photo Stream quite the thrilling mix of photos, test images, and screenshots of those test images. Not quite the same emotional impact when playing slideshows for family.)

2.20 Photo Stream, shown in the Photos app

Photo Stream is great because you don't have to do anything special other than enable the service. (In the iPad's Settings app, tap the iCloud button, tap Photo Stream in the right column, and then flick the My Photo Stream switch to On.) As long as you're connected to the Internet via Wi-Fi, the photos copy automatically to Apple's servers.

Photo Stream stores just 1000 pictures on the iPad. Once you reach that thousandth photo, the oldest images in the stream are removed in favor of new ones. On the iCloud servers, 30 days of photos are saved, giving you plenty of time to connect using your computer and download the pictures. The photos on your computer aren't deleted.

If you do want to make sure a few photos stick around on the device past the thousand mark, copy them from the Photo Stream to an album.

1. On the iPad, open the Photos app and tap the Photo Stream button.

2. Tap the My Photo Stream album. (It's possible to create additional albums, called Shared Photo Streams; see Chapter 8.)

3. Tap the Edit button.

4. Tap to select one or more photos you want to copy to an album.

5. Tap the Save button (2.21).

6. Tap Save to New Album, type a name for the album, and then tap Save. Or, tap Save to Existing Album and then tap an album (2.22).

   The photos are added to the album you created or chose.

2.21 The Save options

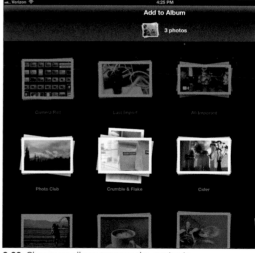
2.22 Choose an album to store the copies in.

Dropbox and Similar Services

Dropbox

SugarSync

Box

If you're not using iCloud, or you want finer control over which photos are uploaded, consider using an online service such as Dropbox. It's a file storage service that has fundamentally changed the way I work on my computers, and it extends its features to the iPad with the Dropbox iOS app. (Other options include SugarSync and Box; I happen to use Dropbox, so I'll describe how it works here.)

On the Mac or under Windows, Dropbox creates a special folder that mirrors its content on the Dropbox servers. Anything you add to the folder is also copied to other devices you've set up with the Dropbox software. Here's a real-world example: All of my active projects are kept in my Dropbox folder. Each time I save a file, it's automatically copied not only to Dropbox's servers, but also to a Mac mini and a Windows PC in my office.

However, the file isn't copied automatically to the iPad (and other iOS devices), because you may not want giant files to be pushed directly to a lower-capacity device. Instead, the Dropbox app is a window to everything stored in your Dropbox folder, letting you browse your files and download the ones you want to view. I can open my article in a text editor on the iPad and work on it, review PDFs, look at photos, and do pretty much anything else as long as I can download a file and own apps that work with the file formats.

Returning to photo backups, the Dropbox app can also *upload* files to your Dropbox. After you install the Dropbox app on the iPad, follow these steps to back up photos.

Automatic Dropbox upload

Like Photo Stream, Dropbox can automatically upload photos from the Camera Roll, even when the Dropbox app isn't running.

1. Open the Dropbox app and tap the Settings (gear) button.

2. Tap Camera Upload and flick the switch to On.

3. Choose whether you want files uploaded only on Wi-Fi connections or also on cellular ones, and then tap the Enable button. Your photos begin to transfer.

Manual Dropbox upload

If you don't want all photos automatically transferred (since Dropbox caps the amount of storage you can use before you need to upgrade to a paid tier of service), you can push images manually.

1. Tap the Dropbox button in the upper-left corner of the screen, if you're viewing in portrait orientation; in landscape orientation, the list of files and folders in your Dropbox folder appears along the left edge of the screen. If you don't see the list, tap the ">" button in the upper-left corner to reveal the folders.

2. Navigate to the location in your Dropbox folder where you'd like the photos to appear.

3. Tap the Upload (+) button and choose Upload Here.

4. In the popover that appears, navigate to the folder in your Photo Library that contains the files you wish to upload.

5. Tap to select the photos (2.23).

6. Tap the Upload button to start transferring the files. When the copying finishes, the files are available at the Dropbox servers and on any of your computers that are connected to the Internet.

▶ **TIP** Dropbox offers 2 GB of storage for free, which is suitable for most people's document needs. Photos, of course, take up much more storage, so you'll want to consider paying for more storage. Paying $9.99 a month or $99 a year gives you 100 GB; $19.99 a month or $199 a year bumps that up to 200 GB; $49.99 a month or $499 a year jumps to 500 GB. That's quite a jump, I know. I use the service enough that the 100 GB range is worth it for me, but I've also been told by reputable sources that if you contact the Dropbox folks directly, you may be able to get less capacity for less money.

2.23 Choosing files to upload to Dropbox

Portable Storage

Until recently, the notion of copying your photos from the iPad to a portable hard disk was science fiction. Doing so makes sense: just offload your photos to a small disk connected via USB. But that would require a level of interaction with the file system that Apple is intentionally trying to obscure; when you're using an iPad, you're focused on tasks, not on shuffling files and figuring out where they're located.

Working with gigabytes of photos, however, begs for the capability to copy lots of files to a small, lightweight storage system. An external hard disk is almost a requirement for shooting on location with a laptop, so why not attach one to the iPad?

As I write this, I'm aware of one product that can make it happen.

Seagate Wireless Plus

Seagate Media

Seagate's Wireless Plus is a $200 portable hard disk with 1 TB of capacity, a battery, and built-in Wi-Fi. Originally marketed as additional storage for the iPad (so you could carry your movie library without having to fill the iPad's internal memory—still a good idea if you are on a trip and don't want to consume your iPad's storage with entertainment), the Wireless Plus can also transfer files from the iPad using the Seagate Media app. (Seagate sells a drive called the Wireless, but it only streams media from the drive to the iPad.)

After you've imported photos into the iPad, do the following to copy photos to the Wireless Plus:

1. In the iPad's Settings app, connect to the Plus's Wi-Fi network.

2. Open the Seagate Media app and make sure the location at the top of the screen says "On [name of your iPad]."

3. Locate the photos to transfer (in the Camera Roll or other album).

4. Tap the Options button (which looks the same as the Share button elsewhere in iOS) in the toolbar.

5. Select the photos you want to back up.

6. Tap the Upload button in the toolbar **(2.24)**. The files begin transferring.

Remember that you're transferring via Wi-Fi, so copying several hundred photos could take a while. This is a good activity to start before you go to dinner, making sure the Wireless Plus and the iPad are plugged into power and not just relying on battery.

▶ **NOTE** In the first edition of this book, I recommended using the Seagate GoFlex Satellite with the app Photosmith to transfer files from the iPad. Although the feature worked when the book was published, the Photosmith developers discovered a serious bug in the Satellite's firmware that corrupted images. So they removed the feature. Unfortunately, Seagate never fixed the bug, but only rolled the feature into their Wireless Plus drive.

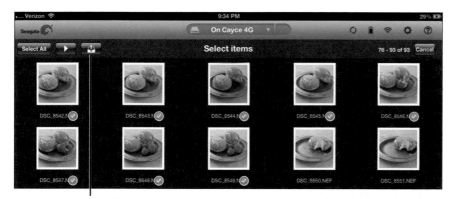

2.24 Copy photos from the iPad to a Seagate Wireless Plus external drive.

Upload button

Dedicated media storage devices

The Wireless Plus is a nifty way of transferring photos from the iPad, but of course the overall goal here is to ensure that all your photos get backed up. If you don't want to wait for the files to copy via Wi-Fi, or if you're generating thousands of images at a time, consider a dedicated storage device like the HyperDrive Colorspace UDMA. At its heart it's a hard drive, but one with slots for nearly every type of memory card and a color screen for previewing photos. It's not cheap, running about $400 for 250 GB of storage (and higher depending on capacity), but it will easily and quickly make a backup while you're on location.

Use the iPad as a Fill Light

Most of this chapter has focused on using the iPad as a photo repository, whether you're importing pictures to review in the field or backing up the images for safekeeping. But there's another use for the iPad that doesn't require any data transfer. That screen is backlit and bright, so feel free to use it on location to throw some illumination on your subject. The screen can't replicate a strobe, but it can be plenty bright, especially in dark situations.

PlainText

The easiest way to set the iPad up as a fill light is to open an app that appears mostly white. Launch Safari and open a blank page, or run something like Plain-Text, a text editor, with a blank document loaded. I made a pure white photo on my computer and imported it into the iPad's photo library, so all I have to do is bring up that image. Then, angle the iPad so the illumination falls where you want it to (2.25).

SoftBox Pro

A more elegant solution is to install the $2.99 SoftBox Pro app. It features several background colors, patterns (for adding custom catchlights), and a brightness control at your fingertips for quick adjustments (2.26). Choose the look you want, tap the screen to remove the controls, and get the shot.

2.25 The iPad, out of frame at left, acts as a fill light with a cyan-colored gel. It also reminds us to monitor caffeine intake among writers after midnight.

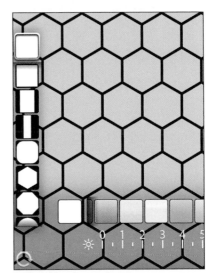

2.26 SoftBox Pro cooling the scene

CHAPTER 3

The iPad in the Studio

An iPad is a great photographer's companion in the field, but it doesn't have to sit dormant when you're back at home or in a studio. The techniques covered in Chapter 2, such as importing photos using the iPad camera adapters or wireless cards or devices, still apply when you're no longer on location. Other possibilities open up when you're not trying to minimize your equipment footprint.

The iPad can work alongside your camera, triggering the camera shutter, providing clients or visitors a window to a photo shoot (without them peeking directly over your shoulder), or even controlling a remote iPhone or iPod touch to capture photos or create stop-motion or time-lapse movies. And with a new crop of wireless accessories, you don't even need a computer (and its cables) in the

Control a Camera from the iPad

Often when you're working in a studio, the camera is tethered to a computer. This arrangement allows you to import photos directly into software such as Lightroom or Aperture, review shots as they come from the camera, and skip the separate import step entirely. So where does the iPad fit in this situation?

If you're shooting products, food, or other compositions that require the camera to remain locked down, you can trigger the shutter, change exposure settings, and more from the iPad without touching the camera. With wireless devices like the CamRanger, CameraMator, and iUSBportCamera, you won't trip on a tether cable as you move around.

An iPad also works well when clients or others want to see your output as the photo shoot progresses. If it's inconvenient to have them hovering over your shoulder, you can hand over the iPad and encourage them to relax on a couch situated a comfortable distance away from the camera.

Capture Pilot HD

Phase One

Tethered Shooting Using Capture Pilot HD

In the first edition of this book, I highlighted onOne Software's DSLR Camera Remote software for controlling a camera that was connected to a computer by cable. Shortly before this second edition was published, onOne discontinued the software.

If you prefer to shoot tethered in the studio but want to incorporate the iPad, look to Capture Pilot HD, which works with Phase One's $299 Capture One software for Mac or Windows. Capture Pilot HD is free to use with Capture One, allowing you (or a client) to view, rate, and tag images as they're captured. A $14.99 in-app purchase unlocks the ability to control the camera and shoot from the iPad. Although it offers many of the same features as DSLR Camera Remote HD, the Capture One software is much more comprehensive, serving as the environment in which you organize and process your photos. Capture Pilot HD also includes a live view, but it works only with Phase One or Mamiya Leaf digital-back cameras.

CamRanger, CameraMator, and Other Wireless Remote Control Devices

As I write this in April 2013, two devices on the market can control a DSLR from the iPad. The CamRanger and the CameraMator each cost $299 and attach to your camera's USB port. I know of two others that are not yet available at press time: Sanho's iUSBportCamera costs $300; and the CamNexus, by the maker of the CameraMator, costs $349 and offers a few additional features, such as controlling multiple devices and building photo slideshows.

CamRanger

All of them can create their own wireless network, to which you connect using the iPad. In general, the CamRanger and CameraMator share many of the features I describe in this chapter, though each has its own quirks. For instance, the CameraMator can hop onto a local Wi-Fi network in addition to creating its own, which lets you access the Internet on the iPad without having to switch Wi-Fi networks. The CamRanger can only operate its own ad-hoc network, which means you're locked away from the Internet while you're using it. However, the CameraMator doesn't display raw files after capture—it will still take the shot, but you can't preview it. (The work-around is to shoot Raw+JPEG.) The CamRanger does display raw images.

CameraMator

CamNexus

By way of example, I focus on using the CamRanger in this chapter, and make notes about the CameraMator where applicable.

iUSBport-Camera

▶ **NOTE** Be sure to check the manufacturers' lists of compatible cameras to make sure the device will work with yours.

Connect the camera and iPad

In the iPad's Settings app, tap Wi-Fi and connect to the CamRanger wireless network; the device's serial number is the network password. If you own a CameraMator, you can also connect solely to its network or set it to recognize known networks:

1. Open the CameraMator app and tap either Remote Camera or Session Preview.

2. Tap the Network Settings option.

3. Set "Join known networks" to On and tap the name of the network you want the CameraMator to remember.

Compose and shoot

In many respects, your digital camera is already a computer, so why not use another computer to control the camera's settings and fire the shutter? In the device's app, use the following controls (3.1). Some items can't be adjusted, depending on the camera model. Using my D90 as an example, I can't change the exposure mode in software, because that setting is a physical knob on the camera. Also, as you would expect, the mode determines which settings are active—in shutter priority mode ("S" on Nikon models, "Tv" on Canon cameras), the aperture can't be set, because that's a value the camera calculates based on the desired shutter speed and ISO.

3.1 The CamRanger interface

A. Shutter Speed. Tap the Shutter Speed button to specify how long the shutter remains open.

B. Aperture. Tap the current Aperture setting to choose an f-stop from the list of possible values. The popover that appears shows only the settings that are available to the current lens.

C. ISO Speed. Tap this button to choose a level of light sensitivity.

D. Metering Mode. Tap to select how the camera calculates exposure.

E. Drive Mode. Tap to set how many shots are taken during a capture, including time delay and remote trigger options.

F. White Balance. Tap to select one of the color temperature presets.

G. Image Quality. Switch between available quality and format options.

H. Auto Focus Mode. Set how the camera determines where to focus.

I. Exposure Compensation. Choose from the range of positive and negative exposure adjustments.

J. Live View. See what the camera is seeing.

K. Movie Mode. Control video recording.

L. Movie Auto Focus. Tap to toggle between auto and manual focus in Movie mode.

M. Capture. Tap this button when you're ready to capture a shot.

► **TIP** The options that are enabled depend on whether the camera is in PC or Cam USB mode. Tap the Settings button, tap Connection, and change the Connection Mode value to PC; that lets you change settings like Mode despite what the camera's physical knobs are set to.

Use Live View

On supported cameras, tap the Live View button to get a live feed of what the camera's image sensor is seeing.

The CamRanger software can take advantage of the camera's auto-focus features: Tap the image preview to set the Auto Focus point, or tap the Focus button at the top of the screen for more specific focus control (Focus Nearer, Focus Farther, and Focus Stacking) (3.2).

3.2 Focus controls in CamRanger

▶ **TIP** Since the image needs to travel across the wireless network from the camera to the iPad, expect a little lag when using Live View. It's not terrible, but it's not as smooth as looking through the camera's viewfinder. If the camera is locked down, that isn't a problem. Shooting handheld action proves to be more difficult.

Use Bracketing/HDR

The remote camera devices tap into your camera's ability to shoot a succession of three photos with different exposures (the current one, overexposed, and underexposed), a feature known as "bracketing." HDR (high dynamic range) images, for example, are created with three or more images at varying exposures. (However, the app doesn't merge the shots into a single HDR image; "HDR" is just shorthand for bracketing.)

1. Put the camera into its manual shooting mode.

2. In CamRanger, tap the HDR button to reveal the feature's options (3.3).

3. Set which variable is locked using the Property control: Aperture, Shutter Speed, or ISO Speed. If Aperture is selected, for instance, the camera will adjust the shutter speed and ISO to achieve the exposure change, leaving your chosen aperture constant.

4. Tap the Start Value button and choose a setting that establishes a decent exposure for the image, as if you were shooting just one shot.

3.3 Bracketing/HDR options

5. Choose how many exposures will fire using the Number of Shots button.

6. Drag the first slider to specify the variance in f-stops between each shot. For example, a setting of 1 would give you an image at the current exposure, one at +1, and one at –1. The higher the value, the broader the difference in exposure will be in the set of shots.

7. Tap the Start button to fire the shots.

Shoot at specified intervals

CamRanger and CameraMator each include an intervalometer, which captures a series of shots at a specified interval. This automation lets you create a series of time-lapse shots.

1. Tap the Timer button (3.4).

2. Tap the Shot Delay button, and choose the duration between shots in hours, minutes, and seconds (up to 59:59).

3. Tap the Number of Shots button, and enter a number in the text field to dictate how many captures are made during the session.

4. To pause before the first capture, set a time using the Initial Delay control.

5. Tap the Start button to start the intervalometer.

3.4 CamRanger's Timer controls

3.5 The intervalometer in CameraMator

▶ **TIP** The CamRanger stores the intervalometer settings on the device, so once you've started it, the iPad doesn't need to be on or even connected.

▶ **TIP** CameraMator's intervalometer uses a Duration slider to set the length of the shooting session and uses the Interval controls to set the time between each shot, requiring less up-front calculation on your part than CamRanger's approach (3.5).

Record video

If your camera shoots video and is a model supported by one of the remote devices, you can switch to Video Mode and direct the video capture from your iPad. As with shooting in Live View mode, you can see what the camera is recording, start and stop the video capture, and tap to auto-focus. However, you may not be able to play back a video file in the software once it's recorded.

▶ **TIP** The CamRanger doesn't automatically save photos on the iPad. Select a shot you've taken, and tap the Save button to copy it to the Camera Roll.

Triggertrap

If $300 is too costly but you still want to control your DSLR from the iPad, the $30 Triggertrap is a great option. It doesn't give you a live view of the camera—in fact, you don't see any photos at all—but it does offer many methods of triggering the shutter. The Triggertrap app is free; the $30 is to purchase a dongle that's compatible with your camera.

Triggertrap

Yes, you can remotely capture a shot of a specific duration. But that's just the start. Triggertrap uses the iPad (or iPhone) sensors to do things like fire the shutter when a loud noise (such as a clap, whistle, or tap) occurs (3.6, on the next page), when you are driving and want a shot captured out the window every 20 km, when a person enters the picture (for cameras that do not offer built-in facial recognition), or even when a magnet is moved near the iOS device.

Triggertrap is also ideal if you want extreme control over time-lapse and long-exposure photography (3.7, also on the next page).

3.6 Trigger the shutter based on noise level.

3.7 Long-exposure control in Triggertrap

Blux Camera and Blux Lens

**Blux Camera
for iPad**

Blux Lens

I've focused on controlling a DSLR so far in this chapter, but if you own an iPhone (or iPod touch, or another iPad), you already have a pretty good camera available. Blux Camera for iPad, which I mentioned in Chapter 1, has a companion app called Blux Lens that enables the iPhone to be a remote camera. As long as both devices are on the same Wi-Fi network, Blux Lens becomes the camera and the iPad acts as the controller.

Choose one to act as the camera and one to act as the remote, and you can then fire the shutter; lock focus, exposure, and white balance; and set a timer. And, of course, it offers a range of filters to change the look of the captured photo.

Mount the iPad

The iPad's portability can sometimes be a hindrance when you're shooting in the studio. Your hands are probably already full with camera gear—you don't want to set that down to pick up the iPad, or have to crane over a tabletop to view the screen without reflections from overhead lights. That's when mounting the iPad is useful.

Although there are no shortages of cases and stands for the iPad, I favor two options: a secure mount that was designed to integrate into a photographer's collection of stands and arms, and a simple desk mount that props up my iPad nearly all the time it's close to my computer. I encourage you to explore the market for options, which change often. For example, if you also dabble in music, a number of attachments designed for performance stands could also work to hold the iPad in place, to set it up as a teleprompter, to play relaxing music for clients or subjects, and for other uses.

Tether Tools Wallee System

The Wallee Connect system from Tether Tools consists of two parts: a case that connects to the back of the iPad (see the next page), and the Wallee Connect, a sturdy adapter that secures to the case and features holes and threads to connect it to tripods, heads, and lighting stands (3.8). The Connect Kit, which includes the case and the Connect, costs about $120.

Tether Tools

3.8 Wallee Connect

Threads for tripods and light stands

Locking mechanism

The Stump

The Stump

Hundreds of iPad stands exist on the market now, ranging from simple plastic kickstands to large suction cups, but there's one that's proved invaluable to how I work. I often want to prop the iPad next to my computer or on a shelf or table near where I'm shooting. The Stump is a $25 angled piece of heavy material covered in rubber that puts the iPad into three positions, in either portrait or landscape orientation (3.9).

It sounds almost too simple, I'll grant you. I received one in a bag of goodies for speaking at a conference and figured I'd toss it fairly soon. However, it's currently lifting my iPad more often than the Smart Cover I bought. Whether it's for during a shoot or for working next to your computer later, the Stump is a great little addition.

3.9 The Stump is simple, portable, and quite useful.

Extend Your Computer Desktop with Air Display

Here's a neat way to take advantage of the iPad's screen real estate when you're back at your computer processing images: Set it up as a second display. Avatron's Air Display ($9.99) communicates between your computer and iPad via Wi-Fi to extend the computer's desktop **(3.10)**. Stash Photoshop panels on the iPad's screen to get them out of the way, or keep email and Twitter windows off to the side, leaving more space for working with your photos.

Speaking of Photoshop, the Adobe Nav app for the iPad can be helpful without invoking screen sharing. When running Photoshop CS5 or later on the computer, Adobe Nav ($1.99) accesses tools off to the side, offering more workspace on your computer.

Air Display

Adobe Nav

3.10 Use the iPad as an external monitor with Air Display.

Make a Stop-Motion or Time-Lapse Video

iStopMotion for iPad

iStopMotion Remote Camera

Since a studio offers a controlled workspace, you don't have to deal with the whims of natural light or environment. Several apps feature an interval-ometer for firing off shots at specific intervals, which can then be combined into a time-lapse video later. But here I want to focus on a clever app that makes the process of creating time-lapse or stop-motion videos easy on the iPad. iStopMotion for iPad by Boinx Software ($9.99) can use the iPad's built-in camera or an iPhone (or iPod touch) with the help of the iStop-Motion Remote Camera app.

▶ **NOTE** Boinx also sells iStopMotion Home for the Mac for $49.99, which is a more comprehensive tool for shooting stop-motion and time-lapse movies.

Create a Stop-Motion Video in iStopMotion

Although you could use the iPad or an iPhone to snap a bunch of photos and then stitch them together later to make a stop-motion video, iStopMotion makes the process much more painless.

1. In iStopMotion, tap the New (+) button to create a new project.

2. Tap the Cameras button at the top right area of the toolbar and choose the front or back camera.

   If you're using another iOS device as a remote camera, first launch the free iStopMotion Remote Camera app there. Then, on the iPad, select the name of the camera device. Lastly, tap the Accept button on that device to establish the connection. The camera's settings screen appears.

3. On the iPad or the other device, drag the Focus indicator to a spot where you want the focus to be locked (3.11). You can also tap the Exposure button at the top of the screen and identify an area on which to base the exposure level.

   ▶ **TIP** You'll want to shoot where the lighting is consistent, but also make sure you set the Exposure indicator to an area of the scene that's not likely to contain moving elements; they'll throw off the color in those frames.

4. Tap Done to exit the camera settings screen.

5. Tap the Clip Settings button (the gear icon) to set playback speed (frames per second) and how the editing environment appears. Tap the Show button and choose the middle option, which uses an "onion skin" mode to show the last frame and a ghosted rendition of the live video so you can see what the next frame will look like (3.12).

6. Set your scene, and then tap the Capture button to take a shot.

7. Reposition elements in the frame.

8. Tap the Capture button to grab the next frame.

9. Continue adjusting your elements and capturing photos until the scene is complete. Tap the Play button at any time to review what you've shot so far.

You can jump back to any frame to re-take it (make sure you line up your elements accurately), or you can delete a frame by selecting it, tapping the Actions button (the wrench icon), and then tapping the Delete Frame button.

3.11 Lock focus in iStopMotion for iPad.

3.12 See the relative position of objects between shots.

Create a Time-Lapse Video in iStopMotion

Stop-motion animations require a lot of work and even more patience to do well. A time-lapse video, by contrast, needs just patience and an interesting enough place to point the camera. iStopMotion can automatically fire off a shot at an interval you choose, ranging from 0.1 second to 99.9 seconds.

1. Set up your iPad, iPhone, or iPod touch where you want to capture action over a period of time.

2. Choose a camera from the Cameras popover.

3. Tap the Time Lapse button to the right of the Cameras button.

4. Make sure Time Lapse is selected under Mode (3.13).

5. Drag the dials to select an interval, then tap outside the popover to dismiss it.

6. Tap the Capture button to start capturing the scene. The button doubles as a countdown timer while waiting for the next shot (3.14).

7. Tap the Capture button again to stop recording frames.

▶ **TIP** Tapping anywhere near the Capture button works, too—you don't have to hit the button perfectly centered.

3.13 Specify Time Lapse settings.

3.14 The Capture button counts the time to the next shot.

CHAPTER 4

Rate and Tag Photos

Even if I were to do nothing else with photos on my iPad, I would want to perform my first round of rating and keyword tagging. I'd much rather spend time in front of my computer editing the photos than sorting them, especially since rating and tagging can be done with the iPad during downtime like waiting for a flight, chilling out in a coffee shop, or sitting on the couch in the evening.

Actually making that possible, however, is a difficult task, which explains why there are only a few apps capable of doing it. The ones I'm focusing on are Photosmith and PhotosInfoPro, which let you rate and assign keyword tags to imported photos, and then export them with the metadata intact to your computer (including direct sync with Adobe Photoshop Lightroom in the case of Photosmith). Several image editing apps also now offer tools for rating and tagging.

Rate and Tag Using Photosmith

Apple introduced the iPad Camera Connection Kit at the same time as the original iPad. In the years since, we've seen all kinds of software innovations with Apple's tablet, but surprisingly, being able to rate and tag photos hasn't quite succeeded until now. It seems like a natural request: Take the images you imported onto the iPad; assign star rankings to weed out the undesirable shots and elevate the good ones; add important metadata such as keywords; and, lastly, bring the photos and all that data into a master photo library on the computer.

Photosmith

Photosmith, in my opinion, finally delivers those capabilities. When you're shooting in the field, you can act on those photos instead of keeping them in cold storage. Back at the computer, that work flows smoothly into Photoshop Lightroom, so you don't have hours of sorting ahead of you.

Import Photos

After you import photos into the iPad using a camera adapter or wireless device (as described in Chapter 2), you next need to bring them into Photosmith. To pull images from the iPad's photo library, do the following:

1. Tap the Import Photos button.

2. Choose an album from your library at left to view its photos (4.1).

3. Select the images you want to import. The checkbox above each group selects all shots in that group; you can drag the Smart Group slider to adjust the groups by their capture times. Or, tap the All, Invert, or None buttons to refine the selection.

4. The default import setting is to copy files from the iOS library to Photosmith's library, which is what I recommend. It occupies more of the iPad's storage, but is more stable than choosing the alternative, which is to link to the files. If you're running short on free space, delete the images using the Photos app after you've imported them into Photosmith.

5. Tap the Import button to copy the photos to Photosmith's library.

Photosmith can also import photos directly from an Eye-Fi card or from an FTP site. You'll find the configuration options in the Dashboard pane.

4.1 Importing photos
into Photosmith

▶ **NOTE** If you used Photosmith 2 and encountered problems, especially with
large photo libraries, you'll be happy to know that Photosmith 3 (in beta at
press time, but which should be available by the time you read this) imports
images in a slightly different way. Before, the app would automatically scan
the Camera Roll and use that as the photo library. To work around bugs in
iOS, the Photosmith developers rewrote the app so photos are stored in
the app's own library.

Importing from ShutterSnitch into Photosmith

As I mentioned in Chapter 2, I prefer to use ShutterSnitch to import photos wirelessly from Eye-Fi cards and other compatible adapters, but the app stores the
images in its own database. That required exporting shots to the Camera Roll, and
then re-importing into Photosmith. However, the developers of both apps have
come up with a grand solution (and even open-sourced the FileXchange method
for sharing images between apps for other developers that want to implement it).
In ShutterSnitch, export the photos using the PhotoCopy option. Choose Photosmith as the destination app, and the photos transfer over.

Rate Photos

As you'll learn in the pages ahead, Photosmith features several ways to organize and group your photos. But let's start with the most likely first action: reviewing and rating the images you imported. The app supports ratings (1–5 stars) and color labels that track with those features in Lightroom. You can also mark photos that don't make the cut as rejected.

To rate photos, do the following:

1. Double-tap a thumbnail to expand the photo in Loupe view. You can also tap the Fullscreen button to hide the sidebar and review each photo larger. Pinch to zoom in or out to view more or less detail.

2. Tap a star rating on the QuickTag bar to assign it to the photo (4.2). Or, if the shot isn't salvageable, tap the Reject (X) button to mark it as rejected. (The photo will still be transferred to Lightroom if you sync it, but it will arrive marked as rejected.)

3. If you use colors to label your shots, tap one of the color buttons.

4.2 Rating a photo in Loupe view

QuickTag bar

4. Use the Rotate buttons to turn photos that arrived with incorrect orientation in 90 degree increments.

5. Swipe left or right to switch to the next or previous photo.

6. Continue until you've rated all the photos you want.

   To return to Grid view, tap the Grid button; the photos are marked with stars to indicate their ratings (4.3).

The values of the stars are up to you. My approach is to rate anything that looks promising (which sometimes means, "Oh hey, that one's in focus after all!") as one star. Photos that strike me more creatively get two stars. On rare occasion I'll assign three stars at this stage, but usually I reserve stars three through five for after I've edited the photos in Lightroom.

Rate multiple photos simultaneously

For an even faster initial review pass, you don't need to enter the Loupe or Fullscreen views. Select the photos you want to rate or categorize in Grid view, and apply the information at once, like so:

1. In Grid view, tap once on a photo to select it. Tap to select others.

2. Tap the rating or color label in the QuickTag bar to apply it to each selected photo.

3. To let go of your selections, you can tap each one again, but there's a better way: Swipe up on the QuickTag bar and tap one of the selection buttons—All, Invert, or None (4.4).

4.3 Ratings and color assignments appear on thumbnails in Grid view.

4.4 The filter controls in the expanded QuickTab bar include buttons to select all thumbnails or none, or to invert the selection.

Assign Keywords

In the interests of speed and convenience when reviewing photos, one task that's often ignored is assigning keywords to the images. On the computer, it's a mundane but important task (especially if you've ever found yourself trying to find an old photo and ended up just scrolling through thousands of shots); on the iPad, it was darn near impossible to do until only recently.

Create or assign keywords

Bring up a photo in Loupe view or select one or more photos in Grid view, and then do the following:

1. Tap the Tagging button in the sidebar.

2. Tap the Keywords field to bring up the Keywords editor (4.5).

3. To create a new keyword, tap the Search field and begin typing. As you do so, in addition to listing matches to existing terms, the text also appears under a Create New Keyword heading. Tap the tag that appears to add it to the selected photo or photos and to the keyword list.

4. To assign an existing keyword, locate it in the list on the left and tap its button. You can also choose from the lists of Recent and Popular keywords that appear to the right.

   To quickly locate a keyword, begin typing it in the Search field at the top of the screen.

5. Tap Done when you're finished.

4.5 The Keywords controls

Build keyword hierarchies

Keywording is a form of organization, and organization varies from person to person. While I prefer a single list of tags, you may be more comfortable with multiple levels of parent and children terms. Photosmith caters to both styles, letting you build keyword hierarchies that Lightroom understands, like so:

1. With the Keywords editor open, tap the Detail (>) button to the right of any tag to set that tag as the parent.

2. Type the name of the child keyword in the Search field. As the child keyword appears under the Create New Keyword section, Photosmith notes that it will belong to the parent tag (4.6).

3. Tap the new keyword to add it to the list and to the selected photo or photos.

▶ **TIP** When multiple photos are selected and some contain keywords that are missing from the others, an asterisk (*) appears on any term that isn't shared by all. To quickly add it to the rest of the group, touch and hold the keyword and choose Apply to All from the group of commands that appears.

Remove keywords

Suppose you mistype a keyword or apply it to a term by accident. To remove a keyword from those already applied to a photo, touch and hold it and then tap the Remove button (4.7, **on the next page**). Or, to just remove a keyword from the hierarchy, swipe left to right over it and tap Delete.

4.6 Creating a new child keyword, "winter," under "farm"

Edit Metadata

Keywords are essential for locating your images later and for assigning terms that can be found in photo-sharing services and commercial image catalogs, but you should also take advantage of other metadata while you're processing your photos in Photosmith.

With one or more photos selected in your library, go to the Tagging panel of the sidebar and tap any field to enter text (4.8). The Photo Title and Caption fields, for example, are used to identify images on Flickr and other sites. The IPTC fields are also important, because they embed your contact information, copyright statement, and job-specific metadata into the image file.

Create metadata presets

Unless you're narcissistic and enjoy typing your name over and over, you don't want to re-enter the same metadata for each photo. Create metadata presets that include all your information, and then apply them to your photos in batches.

1. Select at least one photo in Grid view, or switch to Loupe view.

2. In the Tagging menu, tap the New Preset button.

3. In the drawer that appears, rename the preset at the top of the drawer, and fill in any other metadata fields you wish to save (4.9). For example, you may want a generic preset that includes your contact and copyright information, and an additional one that applies to a specific location or project.

▶   **TIP** Unfortunately, you can't specify keywords in a metadata preset, which would be great for adding tags that you always apply (in my case, "jeffcarlson" and the camera I'm shooting with, like "D90" or "G12"). I'm hoping that capability arrives in a future update.

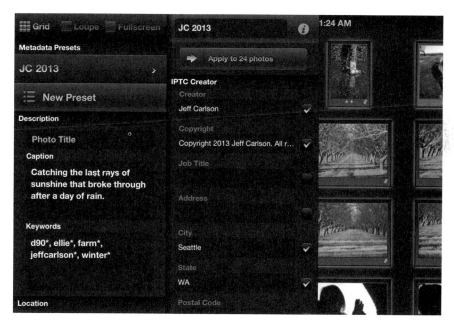

4.9 Creating a metadata preset

To apply that metadata, do the following:

1. In the Tagging menu, tap the name of the preset you created. The information appears in the drawer.

2. Any fields you filled out before are selected automatically; if you want to omit one, tap the checkbox to the right of the field to deselect it.

3. Tap the "Apply to X photos" button to tag the selected photos.

If you want to choose a different preset without applying anything, tap the preset's name in the sidebar to hide its drawer.

You can edit a metadata preset at any time simply by updating the contents of the fields. However, the change isn't retroactive—earlier photos tagged with that preset don't gain the new information.

Filter Photos

Now that you've rated and tagged the photos and applied metadata to them, you can take advantage of Photosmith's filtering tools to customize which images appear based on all that information. Swipe up on the QuickTag bar to reveal the filtering options.

> ▶ **NOTE** Naturally, you don't need to apply every last bit of metadata before you can start filtering your library. Particularly when I want to share something online quickly, I'll do a pass of reviewing and rating my imported photos and then filter that group to view just my two-star picks. But for the purpose of explaining how the features work, it made sense to cover it all before talking about how to filter against it.

Filter by metadata

Here's where that rating and tagging pays off on the iPad. To display photos that match certain criteria, do the following in Grid view:

1. Swipe up on the QuickTag bar to reveal the filter options.

2. Tap the Set Filters button to reveal more specific filter controls.

3. Tap the criteria you wish to filter against (4.10). Selecting a star rating, for example, displays only images matching that rating. You can also filter by color labels and rejected status.

4. Tap Done to apply the filters.

5. To toggle filtering on and off, tap the checkbox to the left of the Set Filters button.

4.10 Using filters to view only photos marked with two or three stars

Change the sort order and criteria

Normally, photos appear in Grid view based on their capture date, with the newest additions at the bottom of the list. To change the order in which they appear, or to list them by import date, star rating, or color label, do the following:

1. Swipe up on the QuickTag bar to reveal the filter options.

2. To toggle the sort order between descending and ascending, tap the arrow at the left of the Sort button (4.11).

3. Tap the Sort button itself to reveal more sorting options.

4. Tap the button for the sorting criterion you wish to use (4.12).

5. Tap Done to go back to the filter options.

4.11 Swipe up on the QuickTag bar to reveal the filter options, including this button for changing the sort order.

4.12 Tapping the Sort button reveals more sorting options.

Filter using Smart Groups

Here's an issue I run into often when importing photos into Lightroom. The pictures on my memory cards tend to span several events, or even days if I haven't been shooting regularly. Lightroom sees the photos as one big collection, regardless of their contents. If I want to split them out into groups—and more importantly, apply accurate metadata during import—I need to bring them over from the camera in several batches.

Photosmith's Smart Groups feature enables you to view those photos in separate batches, adjusted on the fly using a simple slider control. Even if the photos cover one larger event, it's likely they represent distinct experiences. For example, when I'm on vacation I don't usually sit around and shoot in one place. I could be fly-fishing in the morning, sightseeing in town in the early afternoon, hiking later in the day, and waiting for the sunset at a scenic overlook in the evening. (Now I want to go on vacation!)

When I bring the photos I took during that day into the iPad, I get them all in one event based on the date they were shot. Even importing in batches doesn't help, because I end up with just the iPad's Last Imported and All Imported smart collections, not the groupings I prefer (and I can't assign metadata anyway).

A better and faster workflow instead works like this:

1. Import all the photos into the iPad.

2. Import the photos into Photosmith. (This step also lets me cull the obviously poor shots.)

3. Swipe up on the QuickTag bar to view the Smart Groups slider (4.13).

4. Drag the slider to the left to break the library down into finer events (4.14). Or, to group more photos together, drag to the right.

This grouping gives you the opportunity to select ranges of photos by tapping the button to the left of the date stamps. Then you can apply ratings and keywords in batches that better match the grouping of real-life events.

▶ **TIP** The Smart Groups slider doesn't have to be tied to capture dates. It takes its cues from the Sort criteria that are to the left of the slider.

4.13 The Smart Groups slider at its default position

Smart Groups slider

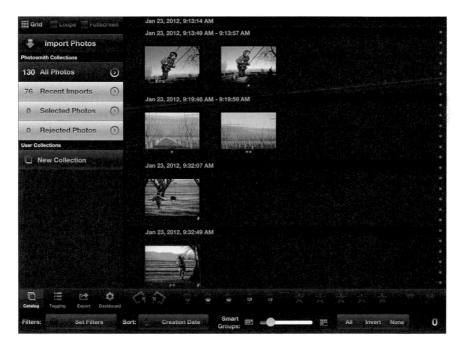

4.14 Selecting a finer setting (drag to the left) breaks the shoot into groups.

Group Photos into Collections

I mentioned earlier that people organize photos in different ways—and that includes how they group photos. For some, having metadata in place is good enough to locate photos using filters and searches. Other people prefer to store images in albums, folders, or other types of digital shoeboxes. Photosmith's collections scratch that itch, giving photos an address within the app where they can be easily found, versus being scattered throughout the larger library. (Collections also play an important part in syncing between the iPad and Lightroom, as I'll discuss shortly.)

Follow these steps to add photos to a collection:

1. Select the photos in your library that you want to include in a collection.

2. If you need to create a collection from scratch, tap the New Collection button and give the collection a name.

3. To add the selected photos to the collection, take one of two actions:

   • Drag one of the photos onto the collection's name in the sidebar; all selected photos will accompany it.

   • Tap the collection's Detail (>) button to view its options in the sidebar drawer, and then tap the Add Selected Photos button (4.15).

Deleting photos from a collection is just as easy: Select the photos you wish to remove, tap the collection's Detail (>) button, and tap the Remove Selected Photos button. You can also delete a collection by tapping Remove Collection in the Detail options pane; the photos in the collection are not deleted from your library.

4.15 Adding selected photos to a collection using the sidebar drawer

▶ **TIP** A faster method of creating a collection is to select the photos you want and then drag them as a group to the New Collection button. Photosmith prompts you to name the collection and then you're done.

Sync with Photoshop Lightroom

And now we get to the whole point of using an app like Photosmith. Rating and tagging is helpful, but if you can't transfer that metadata with your photos to Lightroom, all the work you put into it ends up being futile. Photosmith offers two methods to synchronize your images and data.

Photosmith publish service

Lightroom's Publish Services panel lets you sync photos to your libraries on Flickr, Facebook, and others. Photosmith takes advantage of this conduit, enabling two-way synchronization between the iPad and the desktop. Download the free Photosmith plug-in at www.photosmithapp.com, and install it in Lightroom using the Plug-in Manager.

Any collections you create in Photosmith show up in Lightroom as well, and the photos and metadata remain in sync when you click the Publish button in Lightroom (4.16).

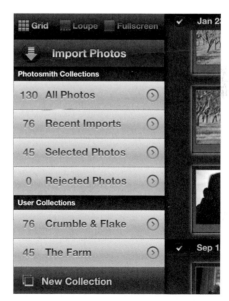

4.16 Collections appear in Lightroom (left) and in Photosmith (right).

Sync photos

To synchronize everything in Photosmith's catalog, do the following:

1. Make sure Photosmith is running on the iPad, Lightroom is running on your computer, and both devices are on the same network.

2. In Photosmith, go to the Dashboard menu and tap the Lightroom button.

3. Tap the Sync Now button to sync the catalog. The photos transfer to Lightroom, and any collections you've made are kept intact (4.17).

4.17 Sync all photos in your catalog.

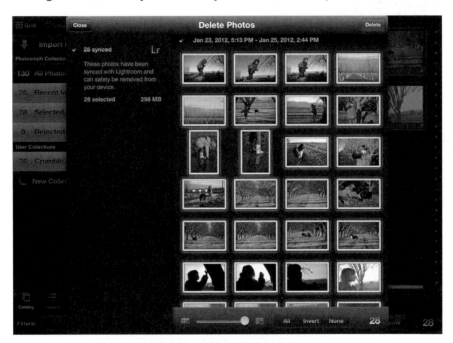

Or, synchronize just a collection. I like this option when I am dealing with a specific project—a single photo shoot or location—and don't want to transfer every new photo from the iPad to Lightroom. Tap the collection's Detail (>) button and then tap the Sync Now button.

▶ **TIP** Before you sync, I recommend adjusting the Local Destination setting in Lightroom for where the Photosmith plug-in stores the files. In my case, Photosmith put everything from my first sync into the Pictures folder on my Mac—a logical assumption. However, Lightroom stores imported photos in subfolders named according to the images' capture dates. In Lightroom, double-click the Photosmith publish service in the Publish Services pane to reveal its settings. Then, go to the Photosmith -> Lightroom Image Options area and specify where the files will end up in the Local Destination field. If your Lightroom catalog already sorts by chronological folders, choose By Date from the Organize pop-up menu and then select a style from the Date Format pop-up menu.

Apply Develop settings

Does your camera tend to capture everything with a slight color cast? Or perhaps you've hit upon a favorite combination of edits that reflect your photographic style. If you've saved those values as Develop module presets, you can apply them (or any of the built-in Lightroom ones) during the sync process. Since Lightroom is performing the edits, they're non-destructive, so you can change or remove them within Lightroom at any point. Double-click the Photosmith publish service to bring up the Lightroom Publishing Manager, and expand the Photosmith -> Lightroom Image Options section. Then select the Develop Settings checkbox and choose the setting you want (4.18).

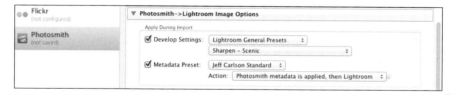

4.18 Apply During Import options

Apply a metadata preset

Earlier, I bemoaned the fact that Photosmith can't save keyword tags in a metadata preset. With help from Lightroom, you can overcome that limitation by applying one of Lightroom's metadata presets at import. If you've already created metadata presets in Lightroom, go to the Lightroom Publishing Manager, select the Metadata Preset checkbox, and then choose the preset you want. In the Action pop-up menu that appears, set how the data will be applied: Photosmith first, Lightroom first, just Photosmith, or just Lightroom.

Sync keywords

In addition to transferring the image files, Photosmith keeps Lightroom's library of keywords up to date every time you sync. This option, also in the Lightroom Publishing Manager, gives you the option of syncing just the keywords applied to the current set of photos or syncing all keywords in the catalog (which happens more slowly).

> ▶ **TIP** Want to speed up Lightroom import? Of course you do! Here's a clever way to copy your photos faster. When you get to your computer, connect the iPad via USB (even if you normally synchronize over Wi-Fi), and use Lightroom's standard import process to pull the photos from the Photo Library; transferring files over USB is much faster than over Wi-Fi. Next, use the Photosmith publish service in Lightroom to sync it with Photosmith (or initiate a sync from Photosmith). The sync copies only the metadata between iPad and computer; it doesn't re-copy the image files.

Photosmith Plug-in Extras

If you'd prefer to transfer photos one-way from Photosmith to Lightroom, use the Plug-in Extras functionality:

1. In Lightroom, choose File > Plug-in Extras > Photosmith, and then choose one of the following options:

    • Sync Keywords: Transfers only the keyword list.

    • Sync Multiple Collections: Transfers one or more collections that you choose.

2. Click the Sync Now (for keywords) or Sync Collections Now (for collections) button to perform the transfer.

3. Click Close to exit the dialog.

Sync photos from Lightroom to Photosmith

Consider this alternate scenario: You didn't get a chance to review your photos in Photosmith while you were out in the field, and you imported them into Lightroom directly from the camera. However, you'd still like to use Photosmith to review the shots, rather than accomplish the task while chained to your computer. The Photosmith plug-in can transfer JPEG versions of your photos (optimized for the iPad's screen if you want, cutting down on storage space and transfer time). Rate and tag them there, and then sync the metadata back to Lightroom when you're ready.

1. In Lightroom, right-click the Photosmith publish service and choose Create User Collection.

2. Enter a custom name for the collection in the dialog that appears (4.19).

3. Click the Create button. If Photosmith is running, an empty collection automatically appears.

4. With the collection selected, click the Publish button. Or, in Photosmith, sync the catalog or just the collection. The images copy to the iPad.

▶ **TIP** When you transfer photos from Lightroom to Photosmith, you don't need to send over the original high-resolution files—the goal is to review the photos, rate and tag them, and then sync just that metadata back. That's especially true if you're shooting with massive files created by cameras like the Nikon D800. The Photosmith plug-in transfers only JPEG-formatted files, at a size of your choice. Go to the Lightroom Publishing Manager (double-click the publish service) and, under Lightroom -> Photosmith Image Options, choose an image size: Full Screen, which matches the resolution of the original iPad 2 and the iPad mini; Full Screen (Retina), the size for the third- and fourth-generation iPads; or Full Resolution, which matches the original photo's dimensions.

4.19 Create a user collection in Lightroom.

After you mark the photos on the iPad, sync the collection or your entire library to update the changes in Lightroom. The same applies if you update a synced photo's metadata in Lightroom: When you sync again, the last-updated version is retained on both devices.

► **TIP** Do you rely on Smart Collections in Lightroom that update themselves based on criteria you feed them? Photosmith doesn't yet support Smart Collections (although the developers say they're working on the feature), but you can achieve similar functionality. In Lightroom, select all photos in a Smart Collection, and then drag them to a Photosmith Publish collection. You'll need to do this again the next time the Smart Collection is updated, but duplicates aren't transferred.

Export to Photosmith

If those aren't enough options, you can also set up Photosmith as an export target. In Lightroom, choose File > Export and then specify Photosmith from the Export To menu. You can specify the image format and size, and you can choose whether to sync keywords for the entire library (slower) or just the keywords in use by photos (faster). The export settings can also be set up as a preset for easier export later.

Export to Other Destinations

As you'd expect, you can share photos to Flickr and Facebook or attach them to outgoing email messages. And you can also copy photos to albums within the iOS photo library, which makes them accessible to other apps on the iPad. You'll find these options in the Export menu.

However, I want to draw attention to three other export options that broaden the usefulness of Photosmith. Although the app was designed to work with Lightroom, you can still export tagged photos to your computer for later processing in other software.

Dropbox

If you're on a robust Internet connection, copy images from Photosmith to Dropbox, which makes them automatically appear on any computer on which you're running the online service.

1. Select the photos you want to transfer.

2. Tap the Export button at the bottom of the sidebar.

3. Tap the Dropbox button to reveal the Export to Dropbox drawer (4.20).

4. At the top of the drawer, choose which photos to send (such as "Send 5 selected photos").

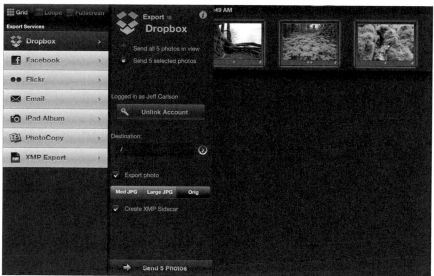

4.20 Send photos to your Dropbox account.

5. Tap one of the upload size buttons (Med JPG, Large JPG, or Orig) if you want to resize the photos.

6. If you want metadata saved in separate files alongside the image files, select the Create XMP Sidecar checkbox (more about this in a moment).

7. Tap the Send Photos button to start copying.

XMP Export

When you're working with JPEG images, additional metadata is written to the image file. But raw images are treated as sacred originals in Photosmith and not changed in any way. To associate metadata with the file, you can export an additional XMP (Extensible Media Platform) file that contains the information and rides alongside the image. So, a raw file named DSC_1234.NEF would have a sidecar file named DSC_1234.XMP that includes the metadata. When imported into most photo management software, the data is combined with the image.

Photosmith's Dropbox option is capable of adding the XMP files during export. If you don't use Dropbox, you can still access the metadata files by tapping the XMP Export button, exporting selected files, and then copying them from within iTunes or via FTP.

PhotoCopy

The PhotoCopy option lets you export photos and their metadata to other iOS apps that support the FileXchange method of sharing images between apps. With images selected, tap the Export Photos button and then choose the app to receive them.

Delete Photos

You're bound to hit the ceiling of how many photos your iPad can store (even if you sprang for the 128 GB model), so you'll want to delete photos from Photosmith. After you've processed your photos and transferred them to your computer, do the following to remove them:

1. Select the photos to delete.

2. Touch and hold the Rejected button in the QuickTag bar to bring up the Delete Photos window.

   Photosmith notes whether the images have been synced to Lightroom or not (to make sure you don't accidentally delete images), and gives you the option of deselecting any shots you want to keep (4.21).

3. Tap the Delete button to remove the images. If you copied them originally from the iOS photo library, those originals still remain on the iPad. If you imported them into Photosmith as links, the links are removed.

4.21 Deleting photos from the Photosmith library

THE iPAD FOR PHOTOGRAPHERS, SECOND EDITION

The Proxy JPEG Workflow

What if, as I describe in Chapter 2, you're recording photos as Raw+JPEG to two memory cards in your camera—one for raw and one for JPEG files? Using a "proxy JPEG workflow," you can import only the JPEG images into the iPad, work with them in Photosmith, and then marry them with their raw counterparts in Lightroom. See http://support.photosmithapp.com/knowledgebase/articles/66161-proxy-jpg-workflow-v2- for more information.

Proxy JPEG
Workflow

Rate and Tag Using PhotosInfoPro

Unlike Photosmith, which focuses on syncing photos to Photoshop Lightroom, PhotosInfoPro takes a streamlined approach that exports metadata in XMP files to be imported into any software that supports the sidecar files.

PhotosInfoPro

Import Photos

PhotosInfoPro reads images in the iOS photo library, so the first step is to choose which album you want to work with. Assuming you've just imported a card's worth of images into the iPad, tap the Library button and choose either the Last Import or All Imported album (4.22).

4.22 Choose an album in PhotosInfoPro.

Rate a Photo

PhotosInfoPro makes it easy to scan your photos and apply ratings.

1. Tap a photo thumbnail to view it larger and to see the metadata your camera applied (4.23).

2. Tap the rating dots below the photo to assign zero to five stars or to mark the image as rejected.

3. Flick right-to-left to view and rate the next image.

I find the default review size to be too small to get a good idea of the image's quality. Tap once anywhere to expand the size (hiding the toolbar at the top) and put the photo against a black background. You can also view the image full screen by tapping the double guillemet (») symbol to hide the sidebar. Pinch-to-zoom works in this view, but the picture snaps back to the screen edges when you lift your fingers.

However, the full-screen view obscures the ratings, so you'll need to tap once on the photo again to reveal them (making the photo smaller again).

4.23 Rating a photo in PhotosInfoPro

THE iPAD FOR **PHOTOGRAPHERS**, SECOND EDITION

Add Metadata to a Photo

To assign IPTC metadata to a single photo, tap it and then do the following:

1. Tap the Metadata button. The Keywords panel appears by default.

2. Type a keyword in the search field to locate a tag you've used previously, or tap Return on the keyboard to create a new one (4.24).

    You can remove a keyword you applied by tapping the Delete (–) button to the right of the word. To delete a keyword from the app's database, swipe left-to-right on it in the Vocabulary list and then tap the Delete button.

3. Tap the tab for another metadata category to edit its information: Headline, Creator, Copyright, Title, or Location.

4. To define a location, type a name in the Search field. Or, navigate the map using your fingers and tap the Drop Pin button in the upper-left corner to set the location in the middle of the map (4.25).

5. To exit, tap the button that hides the keyboard at the bottom right.

4.24 Adding keywords

4.25 Set geolocation information.

▶ **TIP** While you're editing metadata, swipe left or right on the photo to switch between images.

▶ **TIP** When you switch to another image in the Location tab, the map position remains the same. Tap the Drop Pin button to assign the same location as the previous photo.

Add Metadata to Multiple Photos

Of course, you don't want to apply metadata to every photo individually if you're working on a large batch of similar shots. Here's how to tag multiple photos in one swift stroke.

1. In the Album view, tap the Metadata button.

2. Tap to select the photos you want to work with, or tap the Select All button.

3. Tap the Done button to finish making selections.

4. Enter the metadata in the respective tabs (4.26).

5. To exit, tap the button that hides the keyboard at the bottom right.

4.26 Edit metadata for multiple photos.

Export Metadata

PhotosInfoPro exports the metadata you apply in three ways.

- **Master + XMP.** This option sends the original image file plus an XMP sidecar file that contains the metadata.

- **XMP.** Just the XMP files are sent, saving considerable time (especially if you're in an area that does not offer robust Internet access). For example, you could upload the XMP files to Dropbox and then, when you're back on your computer, import the images from your memory cards. You'd then import the XMP files and match them with the photos.

- **JPEG.** The JPEG option writes the metadata into the JPEG file, bypassing the need to deal with XMP sidecar files. However, note that the JPEG route applies an additional level of compression to your images, reducing their quality. Even if the photos were shot on JPEG originally, you'll end up with higher-quality photos by using Master + XMP.

To export photos and metadata, do the following:

1. Choose one image or multiple images; for the latter, tap the Export button in the Album view, select the photos you want, and then tap Done. The Export window appears (4.27).

2. Choose an export option and tap the method you'd like to use, such as the iTunes shared folder, Dropbox, or FTP.

3. In the photo organizing software on your computer, import the image files and XMP pairs.

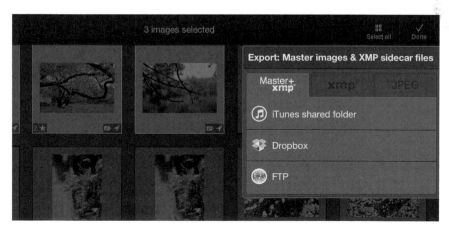

4.27 Exporting multiple photos and their metadata

Rate and Tag Using Editing Apps

I've spent this chapter focused on Photosmith and PhotosInfoPro because they both work with many photos at once. The way I prefer to work, I first review and rate my photos, find the ones that are worth spending more time on, and then bring them into an editing program (on the iPad or on the computer) later. Sometimes it feels as if I can fire off 200 shots just watching dust migrate, so sorting images one at a time just isn't practical.

However, if you're under the gun to process a few shots and share them with a client, editor, or friends online, running them through Photosmith is overkill. That's why some editing apps now offer the ability to edit various metadata and save that information to the exported image file.

Photogene

By way of example, I'm using the image editor Photogene, which I cover in more detail in the next chapter. Although the app contains some metadata support, the pro version adds star ratings and the ability to create IPTC sets that you can apply, which allows you to avoid the drudgery of entering the same information repeatedly.

Rate Photos

Photogene (in its pro mode) offers two methods for assigning star ratings:

*   While you're viewing photos in their albums, touch and hold a photo until an options bar appears, and then choose View Metadata.

*   Open and edit a photo in Photogene's editing environment, and tap the Metadata button.

Tap the General heading in the popover that appears, and then select a star rating (4.28).

4.28 Assign a star rating in Photogene.

4.29 Add descriptive information to the photo's metadata.

Add IPTC Information

Much of the IPTC information that gets embedded with the photo is specific to the shot. In the Metadata popover, tap to edit any of the text fields (4.29).

However, the core data about *you* presumably stays the same, in which case you'll want to create IPTC defaults and sets that you can easily copy and paste to new photos.

Create and use IPTC sets

The advantage to creating sets is that you might want most of the same information (such as contact info) but need something about it tailored for specific uses. In my case, I shoot with two cameras: a Nikon D90 and a Canon PowerShot G12. So, I've set up separate IPTC sets that are nearly identical except for the camera-specific information.

1. In the Metadata popover, tap the IPTC heading and then tap the IPTC Sets button.

2. Tap the plus (+) button to create a new set. Tap the name of the new set to reveal its information fields.

4.30 Make sure
Preserve IPTC is
turned on.

3. Enter the relevant information in the IPTC fields. When you're done,
   tap the IPTC Sets button in the popover's menu bar.

The next time you need to quickly add metadata from one of your sets to
a photo, tap the Metadata button, tap IPTC Sets, and then tap the Use Set
button belonging to the set you created.

▶ **TIP** Using the pro version of Photogene, you can also apply IPTC sets to
several photos in a batch. After you fill in the values in one photo, scroll to
the bottom of the Metadata window and tap the Copy IPTC button. Then,
when viewing your library, tap the Select\Collage button. Tap to choose
one or more images, and lastly, tap the Paste IPTC button.

Export IPTC Information

When you're ready to export the photo, make sure the IPTC data goes
along with it. Tap the Export button and set the Preserve IPTC switch to
On (4.30). The information is written into the file that gets exported.

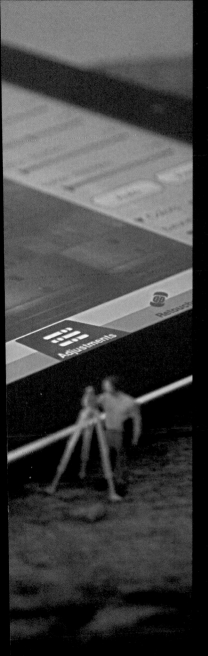

CHAPTER 5

Edit Photos on the iPad

So far, I've focused mostly on moving photos around—importing them into the iPad, organizing them, and getting them onto your computer. And if the iPad were nothing more than a glorified picture frame, that would be fine. But, of course, it's a powerful image editor, too. A rich array of apps can manipulate pixels in all sorts of ways: apply premade filters to simulate other cameras or eras, correct color and tone, retouch to fix blemishes and other oddities, and much more. Image editing tools on the iPad are especially helpful when you want to share photos soon after importing them, before you're back at a desktop computer.

In this chapter, I focus on common photo adjustments using a handful of representative apps. In practice, I use iPhoto, Snapseed, Photogene, and Photoshop Touch interchangeably, depending on how I want an image to appear, so I walk through making edits in those apps. If you already have a favorite alternative, you'll find similar controls for accomplishing the tasks I mention. I also include a few specialized apps, such as piRAWnha for editing raw files directly and Handy Photo for removing blemishes or objects from a scene.

Make Photo Adjustments

In an ideal world, every photo I capture would be perfect in-camera, but that's just not the case. (It's a worthy goal to strive for, however—the less work you have to do to an image later, the better.) Most pictures can benefit from a little tinkering in a few areas. Here are the typical areas I focus on when I want to edit an image. Some of these won't apply in all cases, or may not be needed at all, depending on the image.

- **Recompose.** I'm pulling a few concepts under this heading because they each change the boundary of a photo. Cropping is often done to exclude distracting elements at the edges of the frame or to "zoom in" on a subject, but it's also often used to move a subject away from the center of the image for better visual interest.

- **Adjust tone.** Several tools affect a photo's tone: exposure, brightness, contrast, levels, curves, and more, depending on the software. Adjusting tone can usually restore detail to underexposed areas or add definition to a photo that's overly bright.

- **Adjust color.** Color usually gets edited when adjusting tone, but color-specific adjustments exist that can help photos. Changing the white balance (color temperature) can remove color casts or bring warmth to cloudy scenes, while saturation controls boost or reduce overall color intensity. Some apps also offer a vibrance control, which affects saturation but preserves skin tones (no sense kicking up the saturation if the people in your photo end up looking like Oompa Loompas).

- **Make specific fixes.** Some photos need isolated adjustments: fixing red-eye, spot-retouching, sharpening, and the like.

- **Apply creative presets.** Most adjustment apps include preset filters that approximate the looks of other cameras, add borders or "grunge" effects, or evoke aged film stock.

- ▶ **NOTE** Keep in mind that when you edit a raw photo on the iPad, you're making adjustments to a JPEG preview (or, if you originally shot Raw+JPEG format, the higher-quality JPEG version of the photo). That means you won't get the full advantage of manipulating the raw file, which usually yields better recovery in underexposed or overexposed areas. The exception is if you use an app, such as piRAWnha, that edits the raw file directly (explained later in this chapter).

Edit Photos in the Photos App

I highlight working in third-party apps because they offer more features, but Apple's built-in Photos app also includes a few basic editing tools. Tap a photo to view it full-screen, and then tap the Edit button to reveal the following controls:

- **Crop.** Tap the Crop button to enter the Crop and Straighten editor, and then do the following:

    1. Drag the corner handles or the edges of the overlay to redefine the visible area of the photo.

    2. Drag the middle of the photo to reposition the image within the crop area.

    3. If you want to crop the image to a specific aspect ratio, tap the Constrain button and choose an option in the popover that appears. Further adjustments to the overlay don't adhere to that constraint, though; you need to crop and then constrain again if you want to tweak the border.

    4. To straighten the image, press two fingers against the screen and rotate them left or right, like you're turning a radio dial. (You may need to zoom in first, to provide enough padding for the image to fully fill the crop area.) A faint yellow grid appears to help you align objects in the scene (5.1).

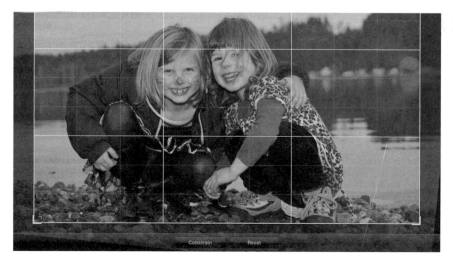

5.1 Grid lines help straighten the photo.

- **Rotate.** If a photo was imported sideways or upside down, tap the Rotate button to turn the entire image 90 degrees counterclockwise.

- **Enhance.** Tap the Enhance button to let the Photos app automatically apply tone and color correction.

- **Red-Eye.** If people or animals have an evil glare about them, tap the Red-Eye button and then tap the affected red eyes to correct them. It's helpful to first zoom in (pinch outward), but the app does a good job of identifying eyes even if you don't tap right in the middle of them.

When you're finished making edits, tap the Save button. Or, tap Cancel to discard the changes. Even after you've saved the picture, you can always resurrect the original version by tapping the Revert to Original button, followed by the Save button (the latter because you need to save the fact that you removed the edits).

Edit Photos in Snapseed

Snapseed

Snapseed differentiates itself from others in this field with an innovative interface that often makes me turn to it just because it's great to use. Conceived for touchscreen interaction, Snapseed doesn't try to be Photoshop in its approach to editing photos. Instead, it uses immediately familiar swiping gestures for choosing which edits to apply and for controlling their intensities.

To get started in Snapseed, launch the app, tap the Image Source button (the camera icon in the upper-left corner), and choose the photo you want to edit from your Photo Library. Once the image is loaded, tap one of the app's correction modules (5.2).

5.2 Snapseed's modules lead to controls specific to their adjustments.

► **TIP** In any of the Snapseed modules, tap the Back button to return to the app's main screen without applying any adjustments. Or, while you're working, tap the Preview button to see how the edits will look once applied; in some tools, a Compare button appears instead, so you can toggle quickly back to the version that existed before your edits.

Recompose

To change the visible area of the photo, tap the Crop module and then do the following:

1. Drag the corner handles or edges of the selection rectangle to define the image borders.

2. Tap the Ratio button to constrain alterations to a set aspect ratio (5.3). Unlike the Photos app, the Ratio control locks the shape, enabling you to refine the borders at that aspect ratio.

    To switch between landscape and portrait orientation for the selection area, tap the Rotate button.

3. Tap the Apply button to accept the cropped area and return to the app's main screen.

5.3 The crop area is constrained to the 16:9 ratio.

If you need to straighten or rotate the image, tap the Straighten & Rotate module and do this:

1. Tap the Rotate Left or Rotate Right button to turn the image in 90-degree increments.

2. Drag left or right on the image to adjust the rotation angle, up to 10 degrees in either direction. (Dragging up or down also works.) Positioning your finger farther away from the center of the image affords more granular adjustments.

3. Tap the Apply button.

Adjust Tone and Color

The Crop and Straighten & Rotate modules use controls similar to other apps for their edits, but most of the other tools work in a central "cross" configuration: Drag up and down to select the type of adjustment you want to make, and then drag left or right to increase or decrease the amount of the adjustment. For example:

1. Tap the Tune Image module.

2. Drag vertically to display the available adjustments and select one, such as Saturation (5.4).

3. Drag horizontally to increase or decrease the amount, indicated at the bottom of the screen (5.5).

4. Repeat steps 2 and 3 to choose other adjustments.

5. Tap Apply to save the edits.

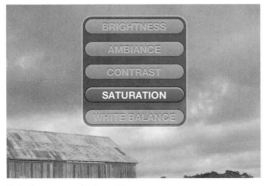

5.4 Choose an adjustment type.

5.5 Drag left or right to specify the amount.

Adjust Specific Areas

Most of Snapseed's tools apply edits to the entire image. When you need to punch up just one area, use the Selective Adjust module. Although it doesn't offer the ability to make precise selections, such as highlighting a certain object in an image, the tool lets you define a feathered, circular area to apply brightness, contrast, and saturation.

1. With an image loaded, tap the Selective Adjust module to open it.

2. Tap the Add button to create an edit point.

3. Tap a location on your image to specify the center of the adjustment.

4. Pinch inward or outward from the point to define the affected area, which shows up as a temporary red mask while you pinch.

5. Drag up or down to choose an adjustment, which is represented on the point by its first letter: B for brightness, C for contrast, and S for saturation.

6. Drag left or right to set the intensity of the adjustment; in addition to the display at the bottom of the screen, the edit point also displays a green border to represent a positive value, or a red border for a negative value, according to the amount **(5.6)**.

7. Repeat as needed to get the look you want, then tap Apply.

▶ **TIP** To make sure you're getting an accurate view of the adjustments you make, turn up the iPad's Brightness setting. Go to the Settings app, tap Brightness & Wallpaper, and drag the Brightness slider all the way to the right. Or, access the control without taking a trip to the Settings app: Double-click the Home button, or swipe up the screen with three fingers, to reveal the list of recent apps. Flick left to right, which displays the Brightness slider as well as music playback controls and the Mute or Screen Lock button. Drag the slider to the right to increase brightness, and then press the Home button to hide the controls.

5.6 To highlight the barn in this photo, I've increased brightness and saturation around the edit point at left (with the light gray radius line indicating the affected area). The edit point at right reduces brightness and increases contrast.

Apply Creative Presets

Half of Snapseed's modules are dedicated to applying creative effects, which follow the same approach as the correction tools. Choose Black & White, Vintage Films, Drama, Grunge, Center Focus, Tilt-Shift, or Retrolux to take a photo in a new direction from the original (the image above was styled with the Drama 2 preset).

▶ **TIP** Most of the presets include a fixed number of styles, but they offer much more variation than you might expect. In Vintage Films, for instance, tap the Texture button and then tap the Properties button to randomly apply texture patterns. Or, in the Grunge module, just drag from left to right to view hundreds of variations in color.

Edit Photos in Photogene

Photogene

You may already be adept at pushing pixels in Photoshop or Photoshop Elements, in which case you'll find Mobile Pond's Photogene for iPad to be a familiar editing environment. It includes traditional tools such as levels and curves, lets you work with layers and masks, and boasts full-resolution image editing. (Some advanced features require a $7.99 in-app Go-Pro purchase, which is worth it if you're serious about editing photos on the iPad. The regular version, at $2.99, is still quite capable for most editing.)

To get started, browse your Photo Library and tap an image to open it in Photogene's editor. As you work, you can tap the Undo button to step back among your edits; or, at any point, tap the Original button to discard all changes.

Recompose

To recompose a photo using the Crop tool, do the following:

1. Tap the Crop tool to reveal the selection area and a side pane where you can constrain the aspect ratio.

2. Drag the selection handles to define the visible area. You can reposition the selection over the image by dragging the area from the middle using one finger.

3. Tap the Crop button in the pane to apply the crop.

4. To dismiss the Crop interface, tap the Crop button in the toolbar.

For images that are a bit (or a lot) askew, follow these steps:

1. Tap the Rotate button in the toolbar.

2. In the Rotate panel that appears, drag the Angle slider to straighten the image (5.7). Photogene applies the change as soon as you let go of the slider.

You can also rotate the image by quarter turns or flip the image horizontally or vertically.

▶ **TIP** To reset any adjustment slider's value to its default, double-tap it.

Adjust Tone and Color

Photogene includes several tools for adjusting brightness, contrast, and color, each of which has its own strengths. The Brightness controls, for example, can brighten or darken an image or pull detail out of shadows and highlights. Or, you may prefer to adjust white and black levels using the histogram, or adjust curves to manipulate separate red, green, or blue channels.

▶ **TIP** While you're editing, touch and hold the A/B icon to the right of the side panel's title to view the uncorrected version of the image.

Adjust brightness and contrast

I often shoot with exposure compensation set to –1 (or maybe a third of a stop) because it results in slightly more saturated colors and, more importantly, reduces the chance that portions of my image will end up blown out to all white. Camera sensors, especially when shooting in raw mode, capture a lot of detail in shadows that might not immediately be apparent. Pixels that are blown out, however, rarely offer any usable image data.

The easiest method is to manipulate the sliders in the Brightness section of the Adjustments panel:

1. Tap the Adjustments button to reveal the panel.

2. Drag the Exposure slider to increase or decrease the photo's overall brightness (5.8).

3. Drag the Contrast slider to enhance the distinction between light and dark pixels.

4. To illuminate pockets of darkness, drag the Lighten Shadows slider; this control also affects the full image, but not to the extreme that the Exposure slider does. Similarly, use the Darken Highlights slider to try to recover overly bright areas.

▶ **TIP** I almost always tap the Auto button to see what the software suggests for a fix. And just as often, I follow that by either tweaking the sliders or tapping Reset and starting over. But viewing the automatic settings helps me determine which areas of the image need work.

5.8 Adjusting exposure in Photogene's Brightness panel

If you're more familiar with adjusting levels in desktop software, scroll down to the Histogram section, where you can drag the left vertical bar to set the clipping point of black pixels (making the image darker) or drag the right bar to specify highlight clipping (making the image brighter). The triangle in the middle darkens or brightens the image's midtones.

▶ **TIP** Tap once on the image to hide all of Photogene's panels and controls for an uncluttered view of the photo. Tap again to make the controls visible.

Some people prefer to adjust exposure using curves, a feature available in the pro version of Photogene.

1. In the Adjustments panel, tap the Show button in the Curves section. The interface appears over the top of the image (5.9).

2. To increase brightness, tap the control point in the middle of the grid and drag it up and to the left. Dragging it toward the lower-right area of the grid decreases the exposure.

3. Tap anywhere on the curve to add a new control point, which you can use to further adjust the tones. For example, adding another point toward the lower area of the curve lets me apply contrast (by compressing the dark values) while retaining the increase in exposure I applied in the previous step (5.10).

4. Tap the Hide button in the Adjustments panel when you're done.

5.9 The Curves interface

5.10 Adding a control point

Adjust color cast

Does your photo look a little green? The adjustment tools can compensate for color shifts as well as exposure values:

- In the Adjustments panel, drag the RGB sliders to increase or decrease the red, green, or blue offsets.

- If you've purchased the pro version of Photogene, bring up the Curves editor and then tap one of the colored tabs to the left to edit just those channels.

- ▶ **TIP** Touch and hold anywhere on the image to bring up a Copy Edits command, which notes the adjustments you've made. Then, in another image, touch and hold to view a bar of options, and choose Paste Edits to apply them to that image.

Adjust white balance

If your camera misinterpreted the existing light as being too cool or warm, you can specify a new value for white balance (also called color temperature). Living in Seattle, I often do this to add warmth to photos taken under gray skies, but cameras can be thrown off by fluorescent or incandescent light bulbs as well.

1. Tap the Adjustments button, and scroll down to the Colors section of the Adjustments panel.

2. Drag the Color Temperature slider left (cooler) or right (warmer).

In Photogene's pro version, you can set the white balance by identifying an area that is white, black, or neutral:

1. Scroll down to the Colors section of the Adjustments panel and tap the eyedropper icon.

2. Touch and hold on your image to bring up a zoomed-in loupe, and then drag to locate a neutral color (5.11).

3. Lift your finger; Photogene picks a Color Temperature value based on your selection.

Adjust saturation and vibrance

To boost or pull back the color in your image, drag the Saturation slider. However, to retain skin tone, the Vibrance slider might give better results.

5.11 Use the Color Temperature loupe in the pro version of Photogene to set white balance.

Apply Selective Edits

You won't always want to apply adjustments to the entire image. Photo-gene's Retouches category of tools includes a healing brush but also masking overlays that let you paint areas to be adjusted. For example, use the Dodge tool to brighten an area, or enhance the depth of a photo by applying the Blur tool to its background. The pro version of the software lets you adjust exposure, saturation, contrast, color temperature, and RGB offset values in areas you paint.

1. Tap the Retouches button in the toolbar.

2. Tap one of the Masking Overlays tools.

3. Set the diameter of the brush by tapping the Brush button and speci-fying Radius and Feather amounts using the sliders provided. Tap the button again to dismiss the popover.

4. Begin painting the edit onto the photo by dragging (5.12). To erase an area you've painted, tap the Erase button; or, easier, tap once on the photo to switch between the Paint and Erase tools.

    Normally, you see the effect that painting produces as you work. However, you can also tap the Contour button to view the edit area in translucent red.

5. Tap the Done button at the bottom of the panel when you're finished.

5.12 Apply edits to selective areas. In this case I've inverted the Grayscale tool so I can erase the balloon and reveal its color.

Apply Creative Presets

Photogene offers dozens of presets: Tap the Presets button and choose among several categories (Colors, B&W, Vintage, Frames, and Fun). Then, tap a preset to apply it.

What's more interesting is the ability to save your own presets. For example, if you find yourself applying the same amount of vibrance and sharpening to your images, create a preset. After setting those options on a photo, tap the Presets button, tap My Presets, and then tap Save.

Edit Photos in iPhoto

iPhoto shares a name with Apple's photo software for the Mac, but they're really completely different applications. iPhoto for iOS is optimized for a touch interface and includes features not found on the Mac.

To start editing a photo, select it and tap the Edit button; the editing tools appear at the bottom of the screen. While in editing mode, you can also tap another photo to begin editing it without exiting the mode.

iPhoto

As you work, compare the edits you've made by tapping the Show Original button to the left of the Edit button. Tap it again to return to the edited view. Tapping Undo removes the last edit (or touch and hold to reveal an option to redo), but if you want to start over from scratch, tap the gear button in the lower-right corner and choose Revert to Original.

▶ **TIP** Tap the Show or Hide Thumbnail Grid button to make more room for the photo you're editing. If you don't mind thumbnails along the side, drag the edge of the grid in the top toolbar left or right. That lets you choose between one and three columns of thumbnails. And here's a nice touch, especially if you're left-handed: Drag the top of the grid to move the whole thing to the other side of the screen. That also repositions the tool buttons.

Recompose

I'll be honest, various editors take several approaches to cropping and straightening photos, but I like iPhoto's implementation the best: Select a photo and, in the Editing mode, tap the Crop & Straighten tool.

Straighten the image

If iPhoto detects a possible horizon, it draws a line along it and attaches a rotate button to the right edge (5.13). Tap the button to accept the suggestion and straighten the image. Or, to manually straighten the photo, drag the dial at the bottom of the screen, or touch the screen with two fingers and turn them, to rotate and zoom the image as necessary.

5.13 iPhoto suggests straightening if it detects a horizon line.

> ▶ **TIP** Here's a feature that's fun but almost useless in practice. Tap once on the Straighten tool at the bottom of the screen to highlight it. Now, instead of dragging it to adjust rotation, turn the entire iPad itself clockwise or counterclockwise and use the device's gyroscope. Tap the control again to disengage the gyro.

Crop the frame

To redefine the visible area of the photo, do any (or all) of the following:

- Drag a corner or edge of the image's border to resize the area freely.

- Drag the middle of the image to reposition it within the frame.

- Pinch with two fingers to zoom in or out of the image.

- Tap the Lock Aspect Ratio button (next to the gear button) to keep the ratio of the current frame.

- Tap the gear button to choose from several standard aspect ratios, such as 4 x 3 or 16 x 9. This is often the quickest way to switch between landscape and portrait orientations (5.14).

5.14 Choose from standard aspect ratios.

Adjust Exposure and Color

iPhoto's controls for improving exposure and color include sliders for adjusting brightness, contrast, saturation, and the like, as you might expect. But those are secondary to dragging directly on the photo and applying corrections based on where you touch.

Brightness and contrast

To adjust a photo's tone, tap the Exposure button in the toolbar and do the following:

1. Tap anywhere in the image to reveal the onscreen brightness and contrast controls (5.15).

2. Drag up or down to increase or decrease brightness. (Or, drag the Brightness control in the slider.)

3. Drag left to decrease contrast, or drag right to increase it. (Or, drag one of the Contrast controls in the slider.)

5.15 Exposure controls in iPhoto

Touch and then drag to edit anywhere

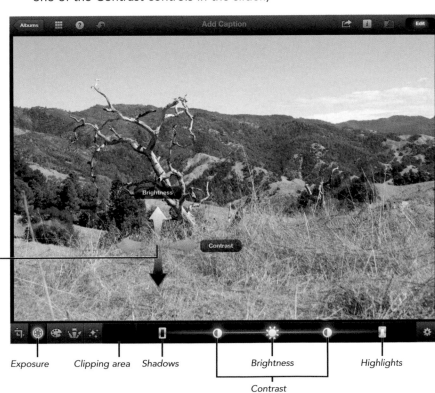

Exposure   Clipping area   Shadows   Brightness   Highlights

Contrast

4. To brighten shadows specifically, touch a dark area of the photo to reveal a Shadows control. Or, drag the left-most control on the slider at the bottom of the screen. Extending it left beyond the hairline border clips the black pixels in the image (the area behind the control turns red to indicates clipping).

5. Similarly, to adjust highlights, touch a bright area of the photo to reveal a Highlights control. Or, drag the right-most slider control, optionally blowing out the lightest values to white.

Color

The color controls focus on five key areas: saturation, blues, greens, warmth, and white balance. The sliders with the descriptive icons at the bottom of the screen control the intensity of these attributes, but you can drag corresponding areas of the photo to adjust those values.

For example, dragging from a blue area displays the Blue Skies control (even if you're not editing a sky) that affects all blues in the image (5.16).

5.16 Apply color adjustments based on the area sampled in your image.

To change the photo's color temperature, tap the White Balance button to the right of the Warmth slider and choose one of the white balance presets. For more granularity, tap the Face Balance or Custom buttons and pinpoint an area of the image to sample. (As the name implies, Face Balance is intended to better preserve skin tones when setting color temperature.)

▶ **TIP** Once you've made tonal or color changes to an image, it's easy to apply them to related photos. Tap the gear button and choose Copy Exposure or Copy Color (depending on the tool), switch to a different photo, and then tap Paste Exposure/Color from the same menu. In fact, you can use this technique to apply adjustments to several photos at once. After copying settings from one, touch and hold to select multiple photos (or double-tap an image to select visually similar ones), tap the gear button, and choose the Paste Exposure, Color and Effect button.

Adjust Specific Areas

Some photos need just a touch of detail adjusted here and there. Using the Brushes tools, paint adjustments just where you want them.

1. Tap the Brushes button to reveal the available tools (5.17).

2. Tap a brush to select it.

3. Zoom or pan the image using two fingers. When painting areas, it's often easiest to zoom in.

4. Drag your finger on areas to apply the adjustment (5.18). If you paint an area by accident, switch to the Erase tool. Or, tap the Detect Edges button (next to the Erase tool) to help you scribble inside the lines. Sometimes it can be difficult to tell where you've painted. In that case, tap the gear button and enable the Show Strokes option (5.19).

5.17 Each effect is represented by a different brush—except Repair, which is a magic wand.

5.18 Painting the berries brightens them.

5.19 View your strokes as a red overlay.

The tool settings popover also includes a slider for setting the intensity of the stroked areas you've painted. You can also apply a brush's effect to the full image (instead of painting) by tapping the [Effect] Entire Image button; this isn't as useful for a brush such as Lighten (since you could achieve similar effects using the Exposure tools), but is helpful if you select the Sharpen tool to make the entire photo more crisp.

> **NOTE** The results of the Brushes and Effects tools are applied to a virtual overlay of your image. If you add an effect and then decide to adjust the tone or color of the photo, switching to another tool temporarily disables the effect (it's pulled up like a plastic film). The edits reappear when you finish the adjustment.

Apply Creative Effects

You won't find the largest selection of preset effects in iPhoto, but for my money, that's fine. The effects are restrained, not thrown in to see how many levels of visual complexity can be piled onto a photo.

1. To get started, tap the Effects button in the toolbar to reveal the effect categories, displayed as if they're bound like a fan or a Pantone swatch book (5.20).

5.20 iPhoto's array of effects

2. Tap a category to select it and explore its effects.

3. For the Vintage and Artistic categories, tap a thumbnail, such as Sixties or Oil Paint, to apply that effect (**5.21**). (It's helpful to tap the Help button—the question mark—to see an overlay that labels each one.)

4. For the other categories, drag along the thumbnail strip until you find a hue or look that appeals to you.

5. If the category includes other options, they appear to the right of the thumbnails. Add Vignette is most common: Tap it to create the dark halo surrounding the photo, and then pinch with two fingers to specify the size and center of the vignette. The Black & White effects also include the options of adding film grain and a sepia tone (**5.22**).

▶ **TIP** I almost can't believe I'm suggesting this, but make sure your iPad's audio isn't muted when you edit in iPhoto. Many actions have sound effects—like a *ziiip* as the loupe appears or disappears—that are quite well done. If you find them annoying, don't worry: At iPhoto's main Albums screen, tap the gear button and switch the Sound Effects setting to Off.

▶ **TIP** Despite the improved camera in the latest iPads, I'm far more inclined to take photos using my iPhone. The iPad, however, is a much better editing environment. Since iPhoto runs on both devices, it's a cinch to transfer photos from one to the other. On the iPhone, select a photo and tap the Share button. Make sure the iPad is also running iPhoto, and tap the Beam button. Specify which photo to beam (the selected one, or others that may be flagged or favorited), and then choose the name of the iPad.

5.21 Vintage effects (with Help labels visible—tap the ? button to view the labels).

5.22 Black & White effects, with a vignette and grain added (but sepia inactive)

Edit Photos in Adobe Photoshop Touch

This is the real deal: Photoshop adapted for use on a tablet. It doesn't support all of the desktop version's features, of course, but you may be surprised to learn what is there: layers, blend modes, selection tools (including the very cool Scribble Selection tool), custom gradients, and more. So, I'm not going to try to provide a comprehensive overview; instead I'll stick with the common operations you're likely to use most often.

Photoshop Touch

▶ **NOTE** It can't be Photoshop without a little frustration, right? In its attempt to provide a stripped-down tablet app, Adobe has made the interface a little too sparse for my taste. For example, many operations are found under the & menu—yes, an "ampersand" menu. So when I mention that you need to choose Crop under the & menu, it's not a typo.

To get started in Photoshop Touch, tap the New From button (at the bottom of the screen, to the right of the New, or plus-sign (+), button) to locate a photo to work with. It can be a photo that is stored on the iPad or on Adobe's Creative Cloud (if you have an account), or that was captured by the device's camera or downloaded from Google or Facebook. Select an image and tap the Add button.

Recompose

Straightening a crooked photo requires two steps: turning the image and cropping out empty space created by the rotation. While many apps crop automatically, Photoshop Touch leaves that step for you to do. Is the app slacking? Not really. Your photo exists on a layer, and edits you make are applied to that layer. This approach gives you the freedom to bring in an image, adjust it, add another image on a new layer, rotate or resize that, and perform other involved edits.

Straighten the image

1. With an image open, tap the Layer Transform tool (which looks like a cross) to view the transformation options.

2. Drag the Rotation button clockwise or counterclockwise to turn the image (5.23). If your image needs just a small amount of straightening, the tool may snap to 90-degree angles; in that case, turn snapping off by tapping the magnet icon in the toolbar.

3. Tap Accept (the checkmark button) to accept the edit.

5.23 Straighten the photo by dragging.

Snapping

Crop the frame

1. Tap the & menu and choose Crop.

2. Drag the selection handles to redefine the visible area (5.24). If you want to maintain the image's aspect ratio, tap the Lock Aspect Ratio button in the toolbar so that it appears that the chain in the icon is unbroken.

3. Drag the middle of the selection area to move the entire area without adjusting its size.

4. Tap the Accept button to finish.

Rotate the canvas

1. Open a photo that needs to be rotated.

2. From the & menu, choose Rotate.

3. Tap a button to choose rotation: Rotate 90° CW (clockwise), Rotate 90° CCW (counterclockwise), or Rotate 180°. This control is also where you can flip the image horizontally or vertically.

5.24 Crop to define the visible area.

Adjust Tone and Color

So you want fine-grained control over how your image appears? Photoshop Touch has a slider for you.

1. Tap the Adjustments button to reveal the collection of tone and color adjustment tools you can use (5.25).

2. Choose a tool to reveal its controls. For example, Brightness/Contrast offers a slider for each attribute (5.26).

3. Drag the controls to adjust the settings, and then tap the Apply button.

Adjust Specific Areas

One advantage Photoshop Touch boasts over most editors is its array of selection tools. You can draw rectangular and freeform lasso selections, feather the selection borders, and more.

For my discussion here, I want to draw attention to the Scribble Selection tool, and use it to make the background of an image black and white while keeping a foreground object in color. This also lets me demonstrate how layers are an important part of editing in the app.

5.25 The Adjustments menu

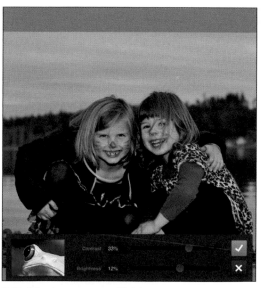

5.26 Adjusting contrast and brightness

1. In the Layers panel at the right edge of the screen, tap the Add Layer (+) button, and then tap Duplicate Layer in the dialog that appears.

2. Next, activate the Scribble Selection tool: Tap the toolbar at the left of the screen to view which tools are available. The Scribble Selection tool is grouped together with the Magic Wand; touch and hold the latter and then choose Scribble Selection Tool when it appears. When a tool is selected, its options replace the column of other tools.

3. Make sure the Keep button is highlighted, because you want to first define the area you want to select. Then, drag to roughly define the area with a green line; Photoshop Touch will do the hard work of detecting edges and making a better selection (5.27). (To refine the selection, pinch with two fingers to zoom.)

4. Tap the Remove button in the toolbar, and then paint the section you want to be outside the selection (the strokes show up in red). As soon as you lift your finger, Photoshop Touch makes the selection. However, if you want to refine the edge, you can continue to draw Keep or Remove strokes.

5. In this example, to keep the lion but remove the background, I chose Extract from the Edit menu (the pencil icon). The image looks the same due to the identical layer below it, but the layer icon reveals a transparent background (5.28).

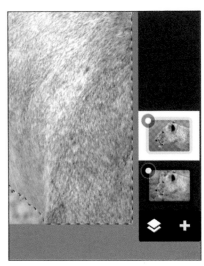

5.27 Using the Scribble Selection tool to define an area   5.28 Background extracted in top layer

6. Tap the Select menu (the dotted rectangle with a gear icon) and choose Deselect to remove the selection.

7. To make the underlying layer black and white, first tap to select it.

8. From the Adjustments menu, choose Black & White. The result is a foreground in color and a background in gray (5.29).

5.29 A quick bit of selection separates the foreground and background.

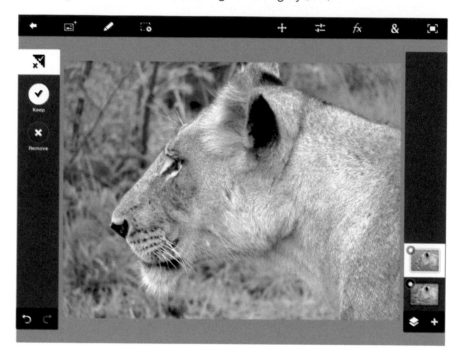

Edit Raw Files Directly

For most of this book, I've referred to this section as an interesting asterisk. In general, the iPad ignores raw files: You can import them, but editing and sharing occurs on their JPEG previews or on the JPEGs that were recorded if you shot Raw+JPEG originals. iOS accepts raw files, but it doesn't support the myriad translators that are required to work with them directly. (I'm sure that's a deliberate design decision on Apple's part. Keeping up with camera manufacturers' proprietary raw formats happens slowly on the Mac because the decoders operate at the system level.)

However, working with raw files is really just a computational hurdle. Two apps, piRAWnha and PhotoRaw (and the free but limited PhotoRaw Lite), act as preprocessors for a photo—similar to the way the Adobe Camera Raw plug-in works in Photoshop on the desktop. If you're working with a dark image, for example, running it through piRAWnha first may tease out detail that another editor might overlook. Then, after exporting the file (as a JPEG), use Snapseed, iPhoto, or Photogene to perform additional edits.

PiRAWnha

PhotoRaw

To be up front, editing raw files on the iPad isn't yet ideal. Expect editing to take a while, even just to make what would be a trivial adjustment on a computer—although the iPad's processor has lots of oomph, the amount of working memory limits how much data can be processed at a time.

PhotoRaw Lite

I prefer the interface of piRAWnha, so that's what I'll use as the example:

1. After you open the app, tap an album from your Photo Library.

2. Tap the image you want to edit.

3. Use the sliders at right for each control to edit the photo's attributes (5.30). As you drag, a preview appears at the lower-right corner.

5.30 piRAWnha's editing interface

> **TIP** Many sliders don't offer much horizontal space to make fine adjustments, but there is a way to choose specific increments: Touch and hold a control to display a popover.

4. Once you've specified all of your adjustments, they aren't immediately applied. Instead, tap the Add to Queue button.

5. Tap the Load Photo button to work on another photo. Or, tap the Export Queue button to process the images waiting in the queue. When finished, the edited JPEG files appear in your Camera Roll.

Retouch Photos

Photo retouching is an area where desktop titans like Photoshop still rule from on high, but some adjustments are possible on the iPad. Although you're not likely to touch up a portfolio of fashion shots using the iPad alone, it's possible you'll want to fix minor blemishes in photos that you plan to share directly from the iPad.

Photogene

Photogene's Heal tool fixes errors by cloning related areas of a photo. I recommend zooming the image to make it easier to control how the edits are applied.

1. Tap the Retouches button to view the Retouches panel.
2. Tap the Heal button.
3. Double-tap the area you'd like to fix (5.31). Photogene adds a pair of retouch circles: One covers the area you selected (and is marked with a gray X), and the other copies a nearby area.
4. Drag the blue anchor points to resize the retouch circle.
5. Drag the center of either retouch circle to reposition it (5.32).
6. Tap the Done button in the Retouches panel to finish.

5.31 Identify an area to fix (the scratch above her eye).

5.32 Clone pixels from a nearby area to retouch the spot.

Handy Photo

Photogene (and other approaches) samples nearby pixels to apply fixes. Another way to tackle the problem is to make software fill in pixels computationally based on the surrounding area. In Photoshop CS5 and later, Adobe calls this "content-aware" healing.

Handy Photo

In the app Handy Photo, Adva Soft uses this type of technology to achieve similar results. It can be especially useful when you need to remove unwanted people or objects from a scene.

In the app, tap the Gallery button to open a photo you'd like to edit, and then do the following:

1. Pinch outward to zoom to 100%, which makes it easier to define the area to be edited.

2. Mark an object to remove by selecting the Lasso tool and drawing around it or by selecting the Brush tool and painting over it (5.33). Use the Eraser tool to refine the edges. You don't need to be too specific about defining the area accurately.

3. Tap the highlighted area. The object you selected disappears.

4. If the result isn't quite to your liking, try painting over the area again.

5. Tap the Main Menu button and then the Save/Share button to save a copy of the photo to your Photo Library, to attach it to an outgoing email, or to share it via Facebook or Twitter.

5.33 As you paint an area to be fixed (in this case, a toy in the background), a preview window appears so you can see the area (which is often obscured by your finger).

Lasso   Brush   Eraser

CHAPTER 6

Edit Video on the iPad

I admit, I look at the title of this chapter and am a little amazed at its implications. Editing video was once something you could do only with a massively expensive infrastructure of equipment. Even as computing power increased (and the cost of software decreased), one still expected to need a high-powered desktop or laptop computer to edit video.

And now here we are, editing high-definition video in real time on a tablet computer. Oh, and using iMovie for iOS, an app that costs just $4.99. iMovie doesn't give you all the features of a desktop video editor, but still: editing HD video on a tablet.

The future is fun.

Work with Projects in iMovie for iOS

iMovie for iOS

Pinnacle
Studio

Every movie you edit is its own iMovie project, accessible from the neon-lit opening screen. To get you started quickly, however, iMovie jumps right into the editing environment after you create a new project. You can return later to grace the project with a name.

At the main screen, tap the New Project button. iMovie takes you to the editing environment (6.1), which works in either the horizontal or portrait orientation.

▶ **NOTE** Although I'm focusing on iMovie in this chapter, it's not the only video editor available for the iPad. Another option to check out is Pinnacle Studio (formerly Avid Studio), which is a more advanced video editor.

6.1 The iMovie editing environment in landscape orientation. When viewed in portrait orientation, the Media Library is hidden and accessible as a popover window.

Media Library

Viewer

Project Settings window

Timeline

Playhead

To give your project a name, do the following:

1. Make any edit, such as adding a clip to the timeline.

2. Tap the My Projects button to return to the opening screen.

3. Tap the title in the marquee to make it editable.

4. Enter a new title, and then tap the Done button on the virtual keyboard.

▶ **TIP** If you create a project and then immediately return to the opening screen, iMovie discards the new project because it has no content.

Choose a Theme

Every movie must have a theme, even if you don't plan to use theme elements. New projects adopt the Modern theme, but you won't see evidence of it unless you specifically choose a themed transition or add a title to a clip. You can change a project's theme at any time. Any themed assets in the movie automatically switch to the chosen theme (which also means you can't mix and match elements from different themes in the same project).

1. Tap the Project Settings button.

2. In the Project Settings window, tap the theme you want to use.

3. Tap outside the window to apply the setting.

Apply a Fade In or Fade Out to the Movie

Instead of starting with the first frame of the first clip, you may want to begin your movie with a fade in from black. The Project Settings window includes a single-switch option for adding fades to the start and end of a project.

1. Tap the Project Settings button to open the Project Settings window.

2. Tap the switch next to "Fade in from black" or "Fade out to black" (or both) to change the setting from Off to On.

3. Tap outside the window to apply the setting.

Open an Existing Project

iMovie keeps track of your saved projects on the opening screen, like you're choosing a video at a stylish multiplex.

1. Tap the My Projects button to return to the main screen.

2. Swipe the project icons until the one you want is highlighted.

3. Tap the icon to open the project.

Add Video to a Project

iMovie for iOS is picky about the video it uses. Basically, if the video came from an iPad, iPhone, or iPod touch, you're golden. However, I've also had success with footage from a few other cameras (such as a Canon EOS M and a Nikon D600, as well as my old Flip MinoHD). If iMovie balks at the video produced by your camera model, you will need to first convert it on your computer. That said, there are several ways to get video into iMovie.

Capture Video Directly

Using the cameras on the iPad, you can record video directly into your iMovie timeline. With a project open, do the following:

1. Tap the Camera button.

2. Set the mode switch to video.

3. Tap the Record button to begin capturing the footage.

4. Tap the Record button again to stop recording.

5. Press the Play button that appears to review your footage. If the clip is acceptable, tap the Use button; the clip appears in the Video browser and at the point in your movie where the playhead was positioned.

   If the clip isn't what you want, tap the Retake button and shoot again.

It's important to detail this approach, because iMovie treats video differently depending on whether it was captured or imported: Video shot by the device stays with the project in which it was captured; it isn't automatically added to the Camera Roll, which is where iOS stores photos and videos that were shot by the Camera app or imported using the iPad camera adapters. If you create a new project, that clip you shot in a previous project won't appear at all.

However, there is a workaround: Move a clip to the Camera Roll by tapping the Edit button and then tapping the Move button that appears.

Import from an iPhone or iPod touch

I'm far more likely to shoot video using my iPhone than my iPad, but even though iMovie also runs on the phone, I prefer to edit on the iPad's larger screen. Following the same procedure for importing photos described in Chapter 2, import media into the iPad's Camera Roll from an iPhone or iPod touch using the Lightning to USB Camera Connector or the iPad Camera Connection Kit.

Add Clips from the Media Library

With a library of clips to work from, it's easy to add clips to your project's timeline.

1. Scroll to the position in the timeline where you want the clip to appear. (This doesn't apply if no clips are in the timeline yet.)

2. If you're holding the iPad in its portrait orientation, tap the Media Library button. (If editing on the iPad in landscape orientation, the Media Library appears in the upper-left corner.)

3. To preview the contents of a clip, drag your finger across it.

4. Tap once on a clip to reveal its selection handles.

5. Drag the handles to define the portion of the clip you want to add (6.2). You can also tap the gray Preview button to play just the selected range.

6. Tap the Add button (with the blue arrow) to add the clip to the timeline.

6.2 Select a portion of a video clip to add.

Edit Video

Editing video in iMovie requires just a few core concepts, which you'll quickly adopt as second nature.

Play and Skim Video

The timeline in iMovie for iOS runs left to right across the bottom of the screen. Tap the Play button to preview the movie in real time in the Viewer.

To skim the timeline, swipe left or right. The playhead remains in the middle of the screen, so instead of positioning the playhead on the video, you're actually moving the video clips under the playhead (6.3).

▶ **TIP** When the movie expands beyond the edges of the screen, touch and hold the upper-left edge of the timeline to quickly jump to the beginning of the movie. Hold the upper-right edge to jump to the end.

6.3 The Viewer shows the current frame under the playhead.

Edit Clips

After adding footage to the timeline, you'll find yourself moving, trimming, splitting, and deleting clips to cut out unwanted sections and create good timing.

Move a clip on the timeline

1. Touch and hold the clip you want to move. It lifts out of the timeline as a small thumbnail (6.4).

2. Without lifting your finger from the screen, drag the clip to a new location in the timeline.

6.4 Move a clip in the timeline.

Trim a clip

1. Tap a clip once to reveal its selection handles.

2. Drag a handle to shorten or lengthen a clip (6.5).

6.5 Trim a clip.

Split a clip

A clip can be added only before or after an existing clip; you can't insert a new clip in the middle of an existing clip. To do that, you must first split the clip in the timeline.

1. Position the clip so the playhead is at the point where you want to split it.

2. Tap the clip to select it.

3. Slide one finger down the playhead from the top of the clip to the bottom (6.6). The clip is split into two, with a transition added between them. (The transition, however, is set to None, so there's no break between clips when you play the video. See "Edit Transitions," later in the chapter.)

6.6 Split a clip.

Delete a clip

Drag a clip from the timeline to the Viewer until you see a small cloud icon appear (6.7). When you lift your finger from the screen, the clip disappears in a puff of smoke.

6.7 Give a clip the Keyser Söze treatment.

Use the Precision Editor

1. Tap a transition icon to select it, and then tap the double-triangle icon to display the Precision Editor (6.8). Or, pinch outward vertically on a transition.

2. Do any of the following to adjust the edit point:

    • Drag the transition itself to reposition the edit point without changing the duration of the surrounding clips.

    • Drag the top handle to change the end point of the previous clip without adjusting the next clip.

    • Drag the bottom handle to change the start point of the next clip without adjusting the previous clip.

3. Tap the triangle icons, or pinch two fingers together, to close the Precision Editor.

▶ **NOTE** It's possible to adjust the duration of the transition from within the Precision Editor. Double-tap the transition to edit its properties.

▶ **TIP** To view more thumbnails in the timeline, pinch outward horizontally with two fingers to expand the clips; pinch inward to compress the sizes of the clips.

6.8 Use the Precision Editor to more accurately set where adjoining clips begin and end.

Edit Transitions

Whether you like it or not, iMovie automatically adds transitions between every clip. Now, before your imagination fills with endless cross dissolves, note that it's possible to have a transition that doesn't do anything at all—it's there so you can tap it and change its settings.

1. Double-tap a transition icon to reveal the Transition Settings window (6.9).

2. At the left side of the window, scroll to choose the type of transition: None (creating an abrupt jump cut between the clips on either side), Cross Dissolve, or Theme.

    The appearance of the latter depends on which theme you chose for your project. To change the theme, tap the Project Settings button and tap a new one, as described earlier in the chapter.

3. At the right side of the window, scroll to choose one of the four preset durations for the transition.

4. To apply the changes, tap outside the window to dismiss it.

6.9 Choosing a transition style and duration

Add a Title

Any clip can have a title, which is an attribute of the clip, not something added separately.

1. Double-tap a clip to view the Clip Settings window (6.10).

2. Tap the Title Style button; the default style is None.

6.10 The Clip Settings window

Clip Settings

T Title Style   None >

📍 Location   Sacramento >

🔊 ————————————●————   ON ⬤

Delete Clip

Tip: Drag a clip out of the timeline to delete.

3. Choose a title style: Opening, Middle, or Ending. The styles depend on the project's theme and are designed for common spots in your movie. For example, Opening is good for titles at the start of a movie and can occupy the entire screen, while Middle typically runs a title at the bottom of the screen without obscuring your video. Of course, you can choose whichever style you want at any point in your movie.

4. Tap the text field in the Viewer, and enter your title text (6.11).

5. Tap Done in the virtual keyboard to stop editing the title.

Add a title to just a portion of a clip

A title spans the entire length of a clip—even if the clip is several minutes long. If you want the title to appear on just a portion, such as the first few seconds, do the following:

1. Position the playhead in the clip where you want the title to end.

2. Split the clip.

3. Double-click the portion you want, and add a title to it.

6.11 Entering text in a theme title

Autumn Farm

Sacramento

Q W E R T Y U I O P ⌫

A S D F G H J K L Done

Specify a Location

The iPad 2 (and later), iPhone, and iPod touch can all embed location data in the photos and video they capture, thanks to their built-in assisted-GPS technologies. iMovie reads that data, too, and gives you the option of using it in titles and, creatively, a few themes.

1. Double-tap a clip to bring up the Clip Settings window.

2. Tap the Location button.

3. If location information was saved with the clip, it appears in the Location window (6.12). To change the location, do one of the following:

    • To use your current location, tap the crosshairs button.

    • To find a location, tap the Other button to search iMovie's database of locations. Tap the closest match to use it.

4. You can also change the label to something more specific, like a neighborhood or restaurant name. Tap the label and enter new text; it won't change the underlying location data. For example, the Travel theme adds a location marker to a map in its Opening title; the marker stays in place, but its label changes (6.13).

5. To exit the Clip Settings window, tap outside it.

6.12 Location settings

6.13 A custom label applied to the location data

6.14 Use the Location line as a subhead.

> ▶ **TIP** In most themes, the location appears as a subhead below the title. If you don't want to announce the location, why not put that text to good use? In the Location window, enter any text you wish to display, even if it has nothing to do with location (6.14).

> ▶ **TIP** As you're working on editing your movie, you can tap the Undo button to reverse the last action. But what if you tap Undo a few too many times? Touch and hold the Undo button, which reveals a Redo button.

Add and Edit Photos

Predictably, iMovie for iOS can import photos as well as video, and even manages to apply the Ken Burns effect to them. In fact, every photo gets the Ken Burns treatment, without an easy way to keep an imported photo from moving.

Photos you've shot using the device or that were synced from your computer can be brought into your iMovie project. As with video, if you captured photos from within iMovie, those images are restricted to the project that was active when you did the shooting.

To add photos to your project, do the following:

1. Position the playhead in the timeline where you want a new photo to appear.

2. Go to the Media Library and tap the Photos button to view available photo albums.

3. Tap an album name to view its photos (6.15).

4. To preview a photo, touch and hold its thumbnail. On the iPad in land-scape orientation, the preview appears in the Viewer.

5. Tap the photo thumbnail once to add it to the timeline.

Edit the Ken Burns Effect

The Ken Burns effect is based on the position of the frame at the beginning and end of the clip. iMovie determines how best to make the camera move from one state to the other.

1. In the timeline, tap a photo you've imported to select it.

2. Tap the Start button to move the playhead to the first frame of the clip (6.16).

3. Position the starting frame the way you wish: Pinch inward or outward to zoom in or out on the frame.

4. Tap the End button to move the playhead to the last frame of the clip.

5. Adjust the image to the way you want it to appear at the end of the sequence.

6. Tap Done. iMovie builds the animation between the Start and End frames automatically as the movie plays.

Disable the Ken Burns effect

Unfortunately, there's no easy control to turn off the Ken Burns effect and just display a static photo. However, a workaround is possible.

1. Tap the Start button.

2. Pinch the image onscreen so you can see all of its edges (zoomed out), and then release it—iMovie snaps it back into place with a minimal amount of zoom applied.

3. Tap the End button and repeat step 2 to let iMovie snap it into place.

4. Tap Done to stop editing the photo.

Edit Audio

One area where iMovie for iOS sacrifices features for mobility is in editing audio. You can adjust the volume level for an entire clip, but not specific levels within the clip; it's also not possible to detach audio from a video clip. Still, that leaves plenty of functionality, especially now that you can add multiple background music clips, include up to three additional sound effects at a time, and record voiceovers. Viewing audio waveforms on tracks is extremely helpful. Tap the Audio Waveforms button to make them visible.

Change a Clip's Volume Level

So that you don't have multiple audio sources fighting for attention, you can adjust the volume level for any clip or mute it entirely.

1. Double-tap a clip in the timeline to display the Clip Settings window.

2. Drag the volume slider to increase or decrease the overall level (6.17). To mute, tap the On/Off switch so it's set to Off.

▶ **NOTE** Whenever a video clip with audio appears over a background song, the song is automatically ducked (made softer). Unfortunately, iMovie offers no controls for specifying the amount of ducking to apply.

Audio Waveforms button

6.17 Change a clip's volume in the Clip Settings window.

Volume slider

Add Background Music

iMovie can include background music, designed for the current theme, that loops in the background. Or, you can add your own audio tracks (with a few limitations). What's unique about iMovie's approach (and this is mirrored in iMovie on the Mac) is that a background music track is a separate type of audio track that operates a bit differently than iMovie's other audio tracks and sound effects. A background song always starts at the beginning of the movie; it can't be pinned to a specific location in the movie.

Add automatic theme music

1. Tap the Project Settings button.

2. Tap the Theme Music switch so it's set to On. (The Loop Background Music option is automatically selected.)

3. Tap outside the Project Settings window to apply the setting.

Add a background music clip

1. Go to the Media Library and tap the Audio button.

2. Choose an audio source (6.18). In addition to iMovie's theme music selections, the Audio window gives you access to your iTunes music library, sorted by playlists, albums, artists, or songs.

6.18 Audio window

3. Tap the name of a song to add it to your project. It appears as a green track behind the video clips in the timeline (6.19).

    ▶ **TIP** Music written for each theme is available to add to any project, not just to movies with those themes. In the Audio window, tap Theme Music and choose any song you wish.

6.19 A background song added to the timeline

4. To add multiple background songs that play one after another, go to the Project Settings window and deselect the Loop Background Music option. You can then add more audio clips. If you don't change that project setting, iMovie replaces any background song when you add a new one.

    ▶ **NOTE** iMovie does not import any music encumbered with Apple's Fair-Play DRM scheme; those tracks appear in the song list, but in gray with "(Protected)" before their names. Apple abandoned DRM for music tracks a while ago, but you may still have tracks in your iTunes library from before the switch. Apple's iTunes Match service (which costs $24.99 a year) enables you to re-download non-DRM versions of your music (which are often better-quality copies at higher bitrates). If you do subscribe to iTunes Match, your music is synced via iCloud instead of through iTunes on your computer, so you'll need to download any songs you wish to use in your projects from within the Music app.

    ▶ **TIP** iMovie considers any audio file less than one minute in length to be a sound effect, and won't add it as a background song.

Aside from the fact that a background song can't be repositioned in the timeline, you can edit it like most clips. Tap to select it, and then adjust its duration using the selection handles; double-tap it to adjust the clip's overall volume. One downside, however, is that you can't apply a fade to an audio clip, so if you shorten the clip, the audio ends abruptly.

Add a Sound Effect

When you want to add a little punch to your audio, consider throwing in a sound effect. Up to three sound effect clips can appear in a section.

1. Position the playhead at the section where you want a sound effect to start.
2. In the Media Library, tap the Audio button.
3. Tap the Sound Effects button to view a list of available effects.
4. Tap the effect you want to use to add it to the timeline (6.20).

6.20 Sound effects appear on tracks below the video.

▶   **TIP** iMovie's automatic assumption that any audio clip less than one minute in length is a sound effect is an annoyance when you want to use a short song to open your movie. But it's also an advantage: You can add any music file that's under one minute—whether its content is a sound effect or not— as a sound effect clip.

▶   **TIP** Using iMovie's audio recording feature, you can record sound effects while you're shooting or anywhere else. See "Add a Voiceover," on the next page.

Add a Voiceover

Most of the time, your videos can speak for themselves. On occasion, though, you may want to provide narration or a commentary track that plays over the footage. iMovie's audio import feature lets you record your voice (or any sound, for that matter) into the timeline.

1. Position the playhead in your movie where you want to begin recording audio.

2. Tap the Record button to bring up the Ready to Record window.

3. When you're ready to start capturing audio, tap the Record button in the window. iMovie counts down from 3 to 1 and begins recording (6.21).

4. Tap the Stop button to end recording. The recorded clip appears as a purple audio clip below the video in the timeline.

5. Choose what to do with the recorded clip: Tap Review to listen to it; tap Retake to record again; tap Cancel to delete the recording; or tap Accept to keep it in your project.

Feel free to record multiple takes, but keep in mind that you can have only three audio tracks in one spot at a time. Also, mute the other takes before you record a new one.

▶ **TIP** To capture better-quality audio, consider using a microphone instead of relying on the device's built-in mic. That can be the microphone on the earbuds that come with the iPhone or even, when connected to the iPad using the Lightning to USB Camera Adapter or iPad Camera Connection Kit, a professional microphone or USB headset.

6.21 Recording a voiceover

THE iPAD FOR **PHOTOGRAPHERS**, SECOND EDITION

Share Projects

iMovie for iOS is designed to easily turn footage into a movie, but it's also intended to take your video and share it with the world (6.22). That could mean saving the finished movie to the Camera Roll for later viewing or for importing into iTunes on your computer. You can also post it directly to YouTube, Facebook, Vimeo, or CNN iReport (but those options are straightforward, so I don't cover them here).

6.22 iMovie's sharing options

Share to the Camera Roll

When you share your project to the Camera Roll, a final version of the movie is created and made available for you to not only watch, but also access from other apps that can read your photo and video library.

1. Tap the My Projects button to return to the opening screen.

2. With the project you want to share highlighted, tap the Share button.

3. Tap the Camera Roll button.

4. In the dialog that appears, choose a resolution to export: Medium - 360p, Large - 540p, HD - 720p, or HD - 1080p. iMovie creates the finished movie and saves it to the Camera Roll.

5. To view the movie there, open the Photos app, locate the movie at the bottom of the Photos list, and tap the Play button.

Send the Project to Another Device via iTunes

This method of sharing an iMovie project is, quite frankly, a weird work-around, but it has its uses. You can export the project itself—not just a rendered version of the movie—for backing up to your Mac, sending to another iOS device for editing, or importing into iMovie on the Mac. It is, however, a fairly counterintuitive procedure.

Export a project to iTunes

1. At the My Projects screen, highlight the project you wish to export and tap the Share button.

2. Tap the Send Project to iTunes button. iMovie packages all the data and resources (including video clips and audio files) and then informs you when the export is complete.

3. Connect your iPad to your computer.

4. Open iTunes and select the device in the sidebar.

5. Click the Apps button at the top of the screen and scroll down to the File Sharing section.

6. Select iMovie in the Apps column.

7. Select the project you exported (6.23) and click the Save To button. Specify a location, such as the Desktop.

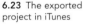
6.23 The exported project in iTunes

Import the project into iMovie on another iOS device

1. Connect the other device to iTunes and select it in the sidebar.

2. Go to the Apps screen, scroll down to the File Sharing section, and select iMovie in the Apps column.

3. Click the Add button and locate the project file you exported in the previous exercise. Or, drag the project from the Finder to the iMovie Documents column. (You don't need to sync the device to copy the file; it's added directly.)

4. Open iMovie on the device.

5. Although the project now exists on the device, iMovie doesn't yet know about it. Go to the My Projects screen and tap the Import button.

6. In the dialog that appears, tap the name of the project to import it. It appears among your other projects (6.24).

See? Only 13 steps to move a project from one device to another!

▶ **TIP** This method is also a way to duplicate a project—for example, if you want to save what you've done but try an editing experiment. After sharing to iTunes, tap the Import button to bring a copy back in; it will have a slightly different name.

6.24 The project as it appears on an iPhone after being copied through iTunes

CHAPTER 7

Build an iPad Portfolio

The desire to showcase your photos may have been your impetus to buy an iPad in the first place. The benefits are compelling: You can show off your work on the large screen, where the backlight makes the photos pop. You don't need to create a printed portfolio, which can involve considerable cost and requires lugging it around whenever you're meeting with a prospective client. And you or your client can zoom in to examine photos in detail.

An iPad portfolio also extends your reach beyond an initial meeting. Email a photo to a client directly from the iPad so they have something more than a business card or a print to remember you by. And since you're likely to have your iPad with you at other times, impromptu portfolio viewings are possible wherever you are—airplanes, lunches, or even just around the coffee table with family members.

5 Steps to Create a Great Portfolio

Before getting into the nuts and bolts (or more accurately, taps and swipes) of building a portfolio, let's look at what makes a portfolio successful. It's easy to throw all your photos onto the iPad and use the Photos app to play a slideshow. What makes a good portfolio stand out is how well it's edited. I doubt there's such a thing as a portfolio that's too small, but many portfolios end up being much too large.

1. **Include only your best work.** I know this should seem obvious, but I find that when I'm picking photos for my portfolio, I often consider one because it's a favorite, not necessarily because it's great. That's an important difference. Always think about how best to impress the person viewing your portfolio.

2. **Demonstrate your range.** Choose photos that show a variety of skills and styles, to better help the client imagine what you're capable of, not just what you've done before.

3. **Tell a story.** Even if your photos are pulled from a variety of situations and styles, your portfolio shouldn't come across as if it had been just thrown together. Start and finish with your best images, and give purpose to everything in between. That can be as literal as starting with images that were shot early in the day and ending with those set at night (7.1), or working through the various stages of a wedding (preparation, ceremony, reception). Or consider working through the color spectrum—black and white images first, building to full-color, high-saturation closing shots.

7.1 Tell a story in the portfolio.

THE iPAD FOR **PHOTOGRAPHERS**, SECOND EDITION

4. **Build multiple portfolios.** If you work in several areas, create portfolios for each, such as for weddings, for landscapes, for portraits, and so on (7.2).

5. **Update the portfolio as needed.** A digital portfolio isn't limited by paper. As you create more great shots, add them to your portfolio to keep it fresh. If necessary, rotate out old images to prevent the portfolio from getting bloated or looking dated.

▶ **TIP** Make sure your iPad portfolio reflects your online portfolio. I can almost guarantee that clients will search for your work online on their own time. Make sure your talents are equally represented there.

iPad or iPad mini for Portfolios?

Since both iPad models run the same software, I've treated them equally throughout the book. But for portfolios, I think the larger iPad is the better option. If you're showing off your work to potential clients, the iPad's larger screen and Retina resolution offer a better viewing experience. I won't discount the iPad mini entirely—it's still good for presenting your photos—but the iPad has the edge here.

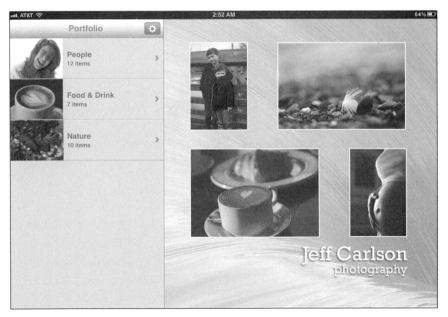

7.2 Multiple portfolios

Prepare Images for the Portfolio

The iPad will dutifully display the photos you add to it, but to make your portfolio look its best, you'll want to prepare the images. Despite having a great screen, the iPad offers no color management. That means the colors you worked so hard to achieve in-camera or on the computer may not match exactly when viewed on the iPad.

You also need to consider the dimensions of the images you transfer to the iPad. Although iOS will scale large images to fit, they may not appear as sharp as you'd like.

Both of these limitations are surmountable. Saving images in the sRGB color space (as opposed to Adobe RGB) provides the closest color fidelity between computer and iPad.

For sizes, the Retina iPad's native resolution is 2048 by 1536 pixels, and the iPad mini, iPad 2, and original iPad screens measure 1024 by 768 pixels. Most apps can handle a 4096 by 2048 pixel size, which provides plenty of resolution to zoom in and appreciate details.

Definitely create some test images to see how they appear on your iPad. Other considerations when preparing the photos include the following:

- **Crop to fill the frame.** To take advantage of the entire iPad screen, you may want to crop the images to avoid empty areas above or below the photo. Personally, I prefer to not crop, so that I retain the same composition in the final photo, but that's more of a general rule than an edict set in stone.

- **Sharpen the image for the screen.** Again, this suggestion is up to you and is worthy of testing. Sharpening the image for the screen can restore some crispness after it's been resized. Since you're outputting to a relatively low-resolution device rather than creating an image for print, I recommend sharpening a little—say, 10 percent—for the iPad.

- **Increase the saturation.** Boosting the saturation of an image can quickly push it into a dangerous realm of Vegas color, but I find that a small push of the Saturation slider (or, better, a Vibrance control if it's available, to avoid messing up skin tones) helps for the iPad's screen.

Using photo editing software on your computer, you can export copies with these characteristics for your iPad portfolio. I'm including a few common solutions here; if you use other software, the steps should be similar.

▶ **TIP** The techniques that follow assume you're optimizing photos for an iPad with a Retina display. The Portfolio for iPad app, which I use as an example later in the chapter, differentiates between Retina and non-Retina devices. If you own an original iPad, iPad 2, or iPad mini, set the maximum size to 2048 pixels instead of 4096 pixels.

Adobe Photoshop Lightroom

When exporting photos from Lightroom, you can specify the size, color space, and other attributes, which can then be saved as a preset. For future portfolio images, you need only choose the preset to get files that are iPad-ready.

1. Select one or more photos to export.

2. Choose File > Export to open the Export dialog (7.3).

3. From the Export To pop-up menu, choose Hard Drive.

4. Choose a location and a method of assigning the filename (such as the image's name or a title you assign).

5. In the File Settings area, set Image Format to JPEG and push the Quality slider to 100. Also make sure the Color Space pop-up menu is set to sRGB.

7.3 Lightroom's export options

6. Under Image Sizing, select the Resize to Fit checkbox and choose Width & Height from the pop-up menu. Set the W field to 4096 and the H field to 2048. (That 4096 value gets applied to the longest dimension, so a photo in portrait orientation will be 4096 pixels tall.) I also recommend selecting the Don't Enlarge checkbox; if the original dimensions are smaller than 4096 by 2048 pixels, enlarging the image can introduce blurring.

7. Scroll down to the Output Sharpening section, select the Sharpen For checkbox, and choose Screen. I keep the Amount value set to Standard.

8. To save these settings as a preset, click the Add button in the lower-left corner of the dialog and give the preset a name. Click Create.

9. Click the Export button to save the file or files.

With the preset created, you can create future portfolio versions by selecting them in Lightroom and choosing File > Export with Preset > [Name of your preset].

Apple Aperture

Apple's photo organizer also offers the ability to create a preset that can output iPad-friendly images for your portfolio. Unlike Lightroom, Aperture does not offer to sharpen the file during export, so you'll need to do that before you export; I recommend choosing Photos > Duplicate Version before sharpening, so you have a separate iteration for export.

1. Select one or more images to export.

2. Choose File > Export > Version(s).

3. In the Save dialog that appears, click the Export Preset pop-up menu and choose Edit.

4. In the Image Export dialog (7.4), click the Add (+) button in the lower-left corner. A duplicate of the currently selected preset is created.

5. Rename the preset to something like "Fit within 4096 x 2048."

6. Set the Image Format pop-up menu to JPEG.

7. Set Image Quality to 12 (the highest).

8. Change the Size To pop-up menu to Fit Within (Pixels), and specify the Width as 4096 and the Height as 2048.

7.4 Aperture export settings

9. Leave the Gamma Adjust slider alone (it should be zero), and set the Color Profile to sRGB IEC61966-2.1.

10. Click OK to return to the Save dialog.

11. Specify a filename and then click the Export Versions button.

Adobe Photoshop

Photoshop's Actions and Automate tools are great for processing a lot of images quickly. Record the steps once to create an action, and you can then use it for other shots.

Create an action

1. Choose Window > Actions to show the Actions panel.

2. Click the New Action (+) button at the bottom of the panel to create a new panel. Give it a name and click Record. Any steps you take within the app will now be recorded.

3. Choose File > Image Size, and set a width of 4096 for landscape images or a height of 4096 for portrait images. (You'll need to create a separate action for each orientation.)

4. Choose Image > Adjustments > Vibrance, and use the Vibrance setting to boost the image's colors slightly.

5. Choose Filter > Sharpen > Unsharp Mask, and set an amount of sharpening you're comfortable with.

6. Save the file by choosing File > Save As, and specify JPEG as the file format, a quality of 12, and sRGB as the intended color space.

7. In the Actions panel, click the Stop button (a square icon at the bottom of the panel).

Batch-process files

With the initial settings recorded, you can batch-process images.

1. Either open the images you want to send to the iPad, or place them all in one folder on your hard disk.

2. In Photoshop, choose File > Automate > Batch.

3. In the Batch dialog, choose the action you created from the Action pop-up menu.

4. Specify where your images are located (a specific folder or images open in Photoshop) in the Source area of the dialog (7.5).

5. Set the location and the file-naming convention in the Destination area.

6. Click OK to process the files.

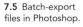
7.5 Batch-export files in Photoshop.

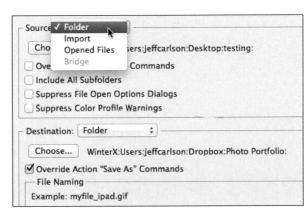

► **TIP** It's also possible to create a droplet, a small application that handles the automation. Instead of choosing Batch from the Automate submenu, choose Create Droplet, and then specify your iPad portfolio action and a destination. Then, whenever you want to prepare some images for your portfolio, you need only drag the photo files onto the droplet.

Adobe Photoshop Elements

The consumer version of Photoshop can accomplish almost everything its older sibling can, and in one dialog.

1. Open the files you want to process in the Photoshop Elements Editor, or group the files in a folder on your desktop.

2. Choose File > Process Multiple Files (7.6).

3. In the Process Files From area, choose Opened Files or specify the folder where the images are located.

4. Specify a location for the converted files in the Destination field.

7.6 Photoshop Elements export settings

5. Under Image Size, select the Resize Images checkbox and enter 4096 in either the Width or Height field, depending on the orientation of the images you wish to process; you'll need to process the orientations separately.

6. In the Quick Fix area, select the Sharpen checkbox.

7. Under File Type, choose JPEG Max Quality from the Convert Files To pop-up menu.

8. Click OK to process the images.

Apple iPhoto

Apple's consumer photo software doesn't offer export presets, but you can easily save a version of a photo that's sized correctly for the JPEG.

1. Select one or more images to export.

2. Choose File > Export to open the Export dialog (7.7).

3. Make sure you're in the File Export section of the dialog that appears, and set the Kind pop-up menu to JPEG.

4. Change the JPEG Quality setting to Maximum.

7.7 iPhoto export options

5. From the Size pop-up menu, choose Custom.

6. To specify the size, choose Dimension from the Max pop-up menu, and enter 4096 in the field.

7. Choose how the file will be named in the File Name setting.

8. Click the Export button.

▶ **TIP** If you have a brochure or other printed work, save it as a PDF and include it in your portfolio. You can then send it to a client via email.

Create Your Portfolio

A portfolio is essentially a slideshow of your photos, and if you want to stick with the basics, you can use the iPad's built-in Photos app to show off the images. But as you're putting a portfolio together, you'll want more control: over how photos are added and organized, over the way they're presented, and over how your client interacts with the work.

Dedicated portfolio apps offer all of those options, and you'll find many programs at the App Store. I've worked with several of them, and Portfolio for iPad is my favorite. I'll use it as the model for building a portfolio on the iPad in this chapter.

Portfolio
for iPad

Using the Built-in Photos App

If you don't want to pay for dedicated portfolio software, you can achieve similar results using the iPad's included Photos app. The trick is in getting the images to appear in the order you wish. In iPhoto or Aperture, create an album that contains the photos, and specify the order there. When you sync, the Photos app honors their placement within that album.

Create and Populate Galleries

Since this is a digital portfolio that will likely change over time, it's important to be able to easily add images to your collection now and later. The Portfolio app groups multiple portfolios into galleries—you can have just one gallery as your entire portfolio, or you can create several. To create a new gallery, do the following:

1. Tap the Configure button (the gear icon), and then tap the Manage Galleries button (7.8).

2. On the Galleries screen, tap the Add (+) button and type a name for the gallery.

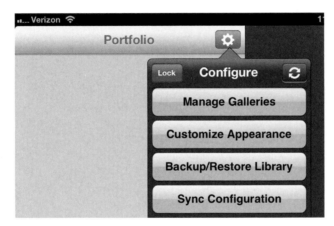

7.8 Configure galleries in Portfolio for iPad.

Repeat the process to create as many galleries as you'd like. If you decide to remove a gallery, tap the Edit button at the top of the page, tap the circular red delete button that appears, and then tap Delete to confirm the deletion.

Add Photos to a Gallery

The best way to load images into a gallery depends on what's most convenient for you. I'm partial to using Dropbox, since I'm a big fan of the service anyway, and it provides a destination for the portfolio-specific images I generated earlier in the chapter. Dropbox also gives me an online backup of my portfolio images, so if for some reason I can't use Portfolio to run a presentation, I can fall back on the Dropbox app. (If you don't use Dropbox, give it a try at www.dropbox.com—the service is free for up to 2 GB of data storage.)

Other possibilities include loading images you've previously imported or synced to the iPad's Photos app via iTunes, fetching files from specific URLs, downloading from the Box service (similar to Dropbox), or using the free Mac application Portfolio Loader, available from the developer. Here's how to do it from the iPad, from iTunes, and from Dropbox or Box.

Load from iPad media

1. With the gallery selected in the Galleries list, tap the Load button (7.9).

2. Tap the Camera Roll button.

3. Using the iOS Photos picker, navigate to an album containing an image you want (7.10).

4. Tap image thumbnails to select which ones to add.

5. Tap the Add button.

6. Tap Done to finish managing galleries.

7.9 Load options

7.10 The window to your photo library

Load from iTunes

1. In iTunes on your computer, click the name of your iPad or the Devices button (if you sync multiple iOS devices); or, if the sidebar is visible, select the iPad there. (If you don't see your iPad, make sure it's connected via a sync cable or a Wi-Fi connection.)

2. Click the Apps category at the top of the window.

3. Under File Sharing, scroll down to the Portfolio app and select it (7.11).

4. Click the Add button at the bottom of the Portfolio Documents pane, and locate the files you want to add. Or, drag the files to the pane from the Finder or from Windows Explorer. The files are copied immediately without requiring a sync operation.

5. In the Portfolio app on the iPad, go to the Galleries screen (as described earlier) and tap the Load button.

6. Tap the File Sharing button (7.12).

7. In the File Sharing popover, select the photos you want to import.

8. Tap the Add button.

9. Tap Done to finish managing galleries.

7.11 Add files via iTunes.

Load from Dropbox or Box

1. On your computer, copy any image files destined for your portfolio to a folder within your Dropbox or Box folder.

2. In Portfolio on the iPad, go to the Galleries screen and tap the Load button.

3. Tap the Dropbox or Box button. A popover appears, containing the contents of your shared folder (7.13). (Or, if you're accessing this feature for the first time, you're asked to log in to your account.)

4. Navigate to the folder in which your images are stored.

5. Tap the thumbnails to select the photos you want to load, and then tap the Add button. The images are copied to the Portfolio app and appear in the gallery.

6. Tap Done to finish managing galleries.

7.12 After transferring files via iTunes, import them in Portfolio.

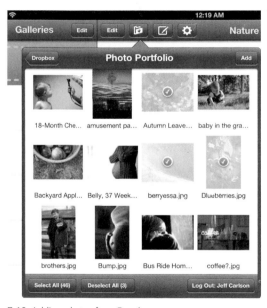

7.13 Adding photos from Dropbox

Edit a Gallery

Here's where you put all that earlier advice to good use. Now that you have a gallery full of images, you need to put them into your preferred order and set a thumbnail for the gallery.

Reorder images

1. Return to the Manage Galleries screen in the Portfolio app.

2. Tap the Edit button above the image thumbnails; the photos appear with close boxes (x).

3. Touch and drag a thumbnail to change its position (7.14). Do the same with the others until the photos are in the order you want them to appear.

4. To remove an image, tap its close box and then tap the Delete button that appears (7.15).

5. Tap Done when you're finished.

7.14 Drag to change the order of photos.

7.15 Remove a photo.

Choose a gallery thumbnail

1. Tap the thumbnail of the photo you wish to use as the gallery's thumbnail.

2. From the popover that appears, tap Set as Thumbnail.

3. In the Choose Target popover, tap the gallery that will get the new thumbnail image.

4. Pinch with two fingers to resize the image to fit the visible area (in the center of the screen, not dimmed); you can also reposition the image by dragging it (7 16).

5. Tap the Crop button to apply the change and assign the image as the thumbnail (7.17).

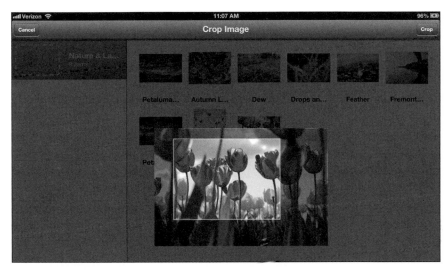

7.16 Specify the thumbnail source.

7.17 Thumbnail changed

Customize the Opening Screen

To personalize the opening screen of your portfolio, the Portfolio app can display three logo screens: one for landscape orientation, one for portrait orientation, and one for an external screen when presenting with a video-out connection like a television or projector.

1. Tap the logo area (helpfully marked with "Tap to customize this image"), or tap the Configure button and then tap the Customize Appearance button.

2. In the Customize Appearance screen, tap a theme's Customize button and then choose Edit Appearance.

3. Tap a component to customize it, such as the image area on the right side of the Classic theme.

4. The Media View window that appears lists specific sizes for landscape and portrait images. In separate photo editing software, create a set of images, in those sizes, that will act as a virtual cover for the portfolio. (You can use any photo, but this area is an opportunity for displaying a logo or other branding.)

5. Tap the Landscape and Portrait buttons and locate the images you want to use (7.18).

6. Tap the Close Customization Panel button, and then tap the Set as Theme button to activate the template. Tap Done.

▶ **TIP** If you don't want to be restricted by the app's logo screen dimensions, create black (or white, or anything else suitably forgettable) versions of the logo images. Then, create a 1024 by 768 logo image and set it as the first photo in your portfolio. You can then bypass the initial navigation and launch your presentation from within the gallery.

7.18 Set custom images for the portfolio's main screen.

Present Your Portfolio

Depending on the client or target audience, you may choose to run the presentation yourself on the iPad, let the photos play in a slideshow, hand the iPad to the viewer, or display on an external television or projector.

Before you begin your presentation, it's a great idea to restart the iPad by powering it off and powering it back on again, which resets the memory. That reduces the chances that the software will stall while shuffling large images in and out of active memory.

Rate and Make Notes on Photos in Portfolio for iPad

The Portfolio for iPad app can also be used to get feedback from someone on the images in your portfolio; for example, suppose you're showing your selects from a photo shoot and want the client to choose a set of favorites. They can rate and comment on individual photos.

1. In a gallery, tap the Note button at the bottom of the screen.

2. Tap the Notes field, and type a comment (7.19).

3. Tap outside the popover to dismiss it.

4. Tap a star in the lower-left corner to assign a rating.

7.19 Rate and make notes in Portfolio for iPad.

Present on the iPad

Presenting your portfolio can be as easy as running a slideshow in the Photos app, but you'll appreciate some of the other features that a dedicated portfolio app can bring. Again, I'll use Portfolio for iPad as an example.

Tap a gallery to view the first photo it contains (7.20). Here, you can tap a thumbnail at the bottom of the screen to jump ahead and view any image in the gallery. For the best presentation, however, I prefer tapping the Full Screen button to view one image at a time. Flick between images by swiping left or right on the screen. (Tap once on the screen to reveal the controls if you want to exit full-screen mode.)

> ▶ **TIP** With the thumbnail strip visible, double-tap a photo other than the one currently displayed; the two photos appear side by side (7.21). Double-tap again to return to the thumbnail strip.

To view an image in more detail, pinch outward or double-tap a photo to zoom in. Double-tap again or pinch inward to see the entire image.

For a self-directed presentation, tap the Play button in the upper-right corner to run the photos as a slideshow.

> ▶ **TIP** If you're handing the iPad to a client, you can lock the editing interface in Portfolio for iPad to prevent them from accidentally editing your gallery. On the Portfolio title screen, tap the gear icon and then tap the Lock button. Specify a four-digit passcode that must be entered to access the editing features. This lock applies only within the app; a client can still access the rest of your iPad by pressing the device's Home button.

Present on an External Display

The iPad's screen is a good size for presenting to one or two people, but if you need to show your portfolio to more, moving the images to a larger display like an HD television or a projector can make quite an impact.

Wired

Connect the iPad to a TV or projector by using an HDMI, VGA, or component cable, depending on the available connections. Apple sells iPad adapters for each type of plug.

7.20 Presentation with thumbnails visible

Full Screen

7.21 Compare two images side by side.

After connecting the iPad to the device, open Portfolio for iPad. If you specified a custom logo page for the largest size, it should appear on the external display. When you enter a gallery, the first image shows up. You can then direct the presentation from the iPad or start a slideshow. (As I write this, it's not yet possible to zoom an image on the external display.)

If you're using an iPad 2 or later, connecting it to the device mirrors the screen, so your viewers can see exactly what you see on the iPad. However, in Portfolio for iPad, only the images appear, not the thumbnails. Swipe to switch between photos, or tap the Play button to start a slideshow.

Wireless

If you have an iPad 2 or later and an Apple TV (second-generation or later, the small black model) at your disposal, and they're both on the same Wi-Fi network, you can display the portfolio wirelessly using AirPlay. To make the two devices communicate, do the following:

1. Double-click the Home button to reveal the iPad switcher bar.

2. Swipe left to right to reveal the brightness, music playback, and volume controls.

3. Tap the AirPlay button, which appears to the right of the fast-forward button. If the AirPlay button isn't there, verify that the iPad and Apple TV are both connected to the same network, that the Apple TV is powered on, and that AirPlay is enabled in the Apple TV's settings.

4. Tap the name of the Apple TV in the AirPlay popover.

5. Set the Mirroring switch to On (7.22).

Now, without being physically tethered to the TV or projector, run your presentation from the iPad.

7.22 Connect to the Apple TV using AirPlay.

Map | Book | Slideshow | Print | Web

CHAPTER 8

Share Photos

Yes, it's true. I do, on occasion, import photos from my camera into the iPad, sort and edit them, and then upload selected shots to photo-sharing services...from my couch. Even when my laptop is just elsewhere in the house, I don't want to retreat to my upstairs office and get into working mode. I want to browse shots from the day, get feedback from my family there in the same room, and put something up that friends can view online.

You needn't aspire to be as lazy as me, but there are many opportunities to share photos directly from the iPad before they inevitably end up on a computer. You may want to post shots from a just-concluded wedding, or maybe a client located elsewhere needs to review and rate images quickly. Several options for sharing your photos from the iPad are available beyond simply syncing the photos to a computer.

0

Upload Images to Photo-Sharing Services

In the early days of the Web (I'm dating myself here), when you wanted to publish a photo online you needed to be savvy enough to upload the image to a server and write the HTML code necessary to make it appear. Now, with popular photo services such as Flickr, Facebook, 500px, and others, you can let the software handle all of that.

Upload from Editing Apps

Most of the photo-editing apps allow you to upload your images directly to Facebook, Flickr, Twitter, Dropbox, and others. The steps are similar in most apps, but since I looked at Snapseed and Photogene in Chapter 4, I'll detail those steps here.

Upload from Snapseed

Snapseed uses the iOS convention of making exporting options available from the Share button; it supports Google+, Facebook, and Twitter.

1. With a photo already loaded in Snapseed's initial screen, tap the Share button (8.1).

2. Tap the name of the service you want to use.

    The first time you share something, you need to log in to the service to grant the app permission to add items to your account. Twitter and Facebook support exists at the operating system level, so if you haven't done so previously, go to Settings and enter your account information. Also make sure that the Allow setting for the app is set to On.

3. Depending on the service, enter a caption, a description, a destination, and privacy options. To share to Facebook, for example, enter a description and tap the thumbnail to choose an album (8.2); if you don't choose an album, it creates a Snapseed Photos album.

4. Tap the Post, Send, or Share button (depending on the service) to upload the image.

8.1 Snapseed's sharing options

8.2 Choose a Facebook photo album.

> ► **TIP** To control who views your photos on Facebook, you need to set up privacy options in your Facebook account. Locate your photo albums, and then click the drop-down menu just below each one to specify Public, Friends, Only Me, or Custom. (Facebook changes its interface often enough that I'm not even going to try to walk you through the steps of locating that control. But once you get to the albums, it should be obvious.)

Upload from Photogene

Photogene offers more services to upload to, and it also gives you options such as image size and, in the pro version, a watermark.

1. Open a photo and edit it as you wish.

2. Tap the Export button (8.3, on the next page).

3. Tap the Resolution\Resize button to specify the image size. In most cases you'll probably want to choose Original, but not always; you may want to upload a smaller version when you don't have much available bandwidth (or maybe you just prefer not to upload full-size photos). The numbers in the Resolution\Resize popover represent the image's longest dimension. Choosing 1024, for example, resizes a landscape photo to 1024 pixels wide but resizes a portrait photo to 1024 pixels tall.

    The pro version of the app adds the ability to set the JPEG quality by specifying the level of compression that's applied.

8.3 Export options in Photogene

4. If you want to strip any metadata you added before uploading, switch the Preserve IPTC option to Off.

5. Tap the icon of the service or feature you want to use. If you haven't previously set up a service, you're asked to log in and grant Photogene permission to add photos.

6. In the service's details panel, enter a title, a description, and other information that applies, including the privacy level.

7. Tap the Share button. Photogene prepares the photo and uploads it.

To Watermark or Not?

I find watermarks distracting, so I generally don't bother to watermark my photos. I want viewers to focus on the photo, not the mark. I'm also not too concerned about getting ripped off—unless I splash a watermark over the entire image, someone stealing the photo can easily remove the mark. However, there are instances when a watermark can be appropriate. Wedding photographers can benefit from having their logo, Web address, or other branding appear on photos that many people will see (the final versions that go to the bride and groom, of course, would be free of marks). You can also use a watermark to indicate that a photo is a proof versus a final version.

Photogene's watermark support (available only after you've paid for the pro version) allows you to specify an image as a watermark and place it on an exported photo. Create your logo or other mark and copy it to the iPad's Photo Library. Then, in Photogene's Export popover, do the following:

1. Tap the Watermark button.

2. Tap Select Image and choose the watermark image you created.

3. Using the sliders in the popover, adjust the opacity of the image and the amount of padding around it (8.4).

4. Choose a position for the mark by tapping one of the boxes in the proxy grid. Note that the preview doesn't accurately convey the size of the mark; it's enlarged to show relative position.

5. Tap the Export button at the top of the popover to return to the rest of the Export options.

6. To include the watermark, switch the Watermark option to On. The watermark appears on the photo that's exported (8.5).

8.4 Setting a watermark

8.5 Watermark applied

iCloud Photo Stream

iCloud's Photo Stream feature began life as a service that automatically copied photos only to your other devices, but it has since added a limited social aspect. When you create a Shared Photo Stream, images are copied to the devices of anyone subscribed to it (and they can get a notification when new photos are added), saving you the trouble of alerting everyone whenever a new picture is added.

1. In the Photos app, view a photo, or tap Edit and select several, and then tap the Share button.

2. Tap the Photo Stream button.

3. In the Add to a Photo Stream window, choose New Photo Stream (8.6). (If you're adding photos to an existing stream, tap its name in the list.)

4. Give the stream a title in the Name field, and optionally enter the email addresses of people with whom you want to share the stream. If you'd like to open the stream to anyone on the Web, turn the Public Website option to On. Tap Next.

5. Optionally enter a comment that will appear with the photo and in the notification subscribers receive (8.7). Tap the Post button.

To add more subscribers to the Shared Photo Stream later, tap the Edit button in the Photo Stream window and then tap the name of the stream. This is where you can also get the URL for the public gallery.

8.6 Add photos to a Shared Photo Stream.

8.7 An optional note becomes a notification to subscribers.

Upload Photos Using Services' Apps

Photo services have been quick to create their own iOS apps, mostly for use with the iPhone so people can upload the shots they take with its camera. For snagging pictures that you've imported and don't need to edit, a dedicated app provides a more direct path from your iPad to your online photo album. In some cases, you can upload photos in batches instead of one at a time.

The first step is to visit the iTunes Store and see if your preferred photo service offers an iOS app. You're also sure to find third-party apps that allow you to view photos and upload them to the services. Here are a few that I use, both "official" and third-party apps.

Flickr

Flickr is one of the largest photo-sharing sites on the Web, and thanks to renewed focus by its parent company, Yahoo, the Flickr app is much better than it used to be—even though it's (still!) not optimized for the iPad. It's easy to upload multiple photos to your Flickr photo stream.

Flickr

1. At the opening screen, touch and hold the Camera button to view your photo library.

2. Choose the album that contains the photos you want to upload.

3. Tap to choose photos, which gain a blue checkmark, and tap Done to continue.

4. Optionally apply edits or filters to the image. Tap Next.

5. On the Details screen that appears, add a title and description, choose whether the shot is public or private, optionally assign the photos to sets and groups, add tags, identify people, and set location privacy (8.8, on the next page).

6. Tap the Upload button to transmit the photos.

▶ **TIP** If you prefer an iPad-native Flickr client, check out FlickStackr.

FlickStackr

Camera Awesome

Camera
Awesome

SmugMug, a popular site for more-experienced photographers, offers an official SmugMug app, but it's geared toward *viewing* photos by you and others. The company ditched its old SmugShot app and now offers Camera Awesome, an app that takes photos and also offers easy upload to one's SmugMug account (8.9).

PhotoStackr 500px

PhotoStackr
500px

The newest entrant in the photo-sharing field is 500px, a site that boasts a great viewing experience and a growing number of professionals. The company's 500px app is a model for how to browse photos on a tablet, but it doesn't offer any way to upload new photos to one's account.

Instead, turn to PhotoStackr 500px, which adds uploading and a few other features to the browsing experience. As with the Flickr app, you can queue several photos to be uploaded together.

8.8 Uploading photos in the Flickr app

8.9 Camera Awesome

Email Photos

A fallback for getting your photos out there is to send them as email attachments. This capability is built into the core of iOS and is available from nearly every app.

I call this approach a "fallback" because, honestly, the current state of email makes it difficult to guarantee that the message will get through. Image attachments are usually large, which increases the chances that the message will stall at a server en route from you to your recipient. Or, the message could be marked as spam and shunted into a person's queue of suspect emails with the usual assortment of get-rich-quick scams and unwanted product solicitations.

Share a Single Photo

Still, email is convenient and widely supported. The iPad uses two ways to share a photo, depending on where you start. If you're in the Photos app, you choose the photo first and then send it via email, like so:

1. Open the Photos app to view your image library. (If you're in a third-party app that offers email as an export option, follow its steps. I'm starting here as if you have just picked up the iPad and want to share a photo from the built-in library.)

2. Locate the photo you want to share, and tap to view it full screen.

3. Tap the Share button, and tap the Mail button in the popover list of options. A new outgoing message appears, with the photo in the body of the message.

4. Fill in the To and Subject fields to address the message.

5. Tap the "Images" text to the right of the Cc/Bcc, From field to specify the size of the outgoing image (8.10).

8.10 The image-size control is almost invisible.

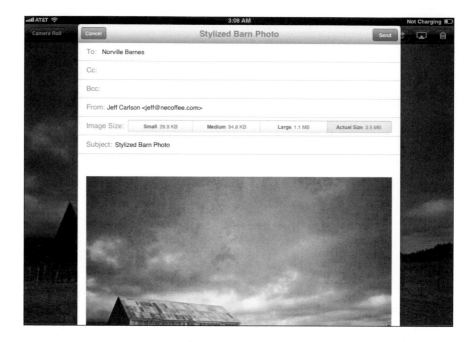

6. Choose one of the Image Size options by tapping it (8.11).

7. Tap the Send button to dispatch the message.

The second way to send a photo by email is to start within the Mail app and attach a photo to the message.

1. In the Mail app, create a new outgoing message.

2. Touch and hold within the message body to bring up the options bar (8.12).

3. Tap the Insert Photo or Video option.

4. Locate the photo in your photo library and tap Use.

8.12 Insert a photo
from within Mail.

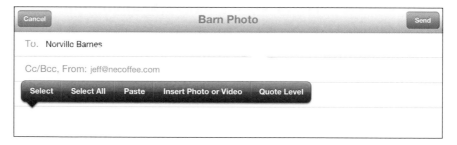

Share Multiple Photos

To attach more than one photo to an outgoing message (without repeating the previous steps for each image), you need a slightly different approach:

1. In the Photos app, open the album containing the images you want.

2. Instead of viewing one full-size, tap the Edit button. The toolbar reads Select Items, and the buttons there change.

3. Tap to select the photos you'll soon be sending.

4. Tap the Share button—this time, a button labeled "Share," not the pervasive icon with an arrow coming out of a square.

5. Choose Mail from the popover that appears (8.13). The photos become part of an outgoing message.

6. Fill in the To and Subject lines, set an image size (which applies to all of the photos), and then tap the Send button.

8.13 Mark multiple photos and attach them to one outgoing message.

▶ **TIP** One advantage to email is that it can act as a workaround when other uploading options fail. My Flickr account, for example, gives me a personal email address. Any image attachment I send to that address is added to my photo stream, which uses the contents of the Subject field as the photo's title and the text in the body of the message as the description. Check your favorite service for a similar option.

▶ **TIP** One way to circumvent email but deliver a photo to a specific person is to use MMS (Multimedia Messaging Service) or iMessage instant messaging. In the Messages app, tap the camera icon to the left of the text field, locate your image, optionally write a note, and tap the Send button (8.14).

8.14 iMessage or MMS is often a faster way to get a photo to someone.

Share Photos Using Adobe Revel

Adobe Revel

As you've no doubt discovered, many photo-sharing services vie for your attention and image libraries. Adobe, digital imaging powerhouse that it is, jumped in with Adobe Revel, which works on iOS devices and in the Revel app for the Mac.

Revel offers a very cool feature that soothes a photography pain point. You can share a library of photos with other people. They can rate the photos, and even use the software's editing tools, without stepping on your versions of the images. So, when I come back from vacation and my wife wants to look through my library and pick out her favorites, I can create a new library for her to browse on her computer or iOS device. I can see her picks in my library, but they don't overwrite mine.

The Adobe Revel software and service is free, with a limit of 50 images per month. Revel Premium service costs $5.99 a month, which removes the limit. It's currently available for iOS and OS X; Windows and Android versions are still in development.

Import Photos to a Revel Library

After you install the app and log in with your Adobe ID (or create a new ID if you don't currently have one), a new library is created. Do the following:

1. Tap the plus sign (+) button to import photos.

2. From the popover that appears, choose Import from Camera Roll.

3. Navigate to an album, and tap to select the photos you wish to import.

4. Tap Done to begin importing the photos. Revel also uploads the images to Adobe's servers for backup and for syncing to other devices on which you install the software (8.15).

8.15 A library of photos in Adobe Revel

Rate and Edit Photos

When I say "rate" in regard to Revel, what I really mean is to mark a photo as a favorite; there are no multiple-star rankings. Instead, tap a photo to open it, and then tap the star button in the lower-left corner of the screen.

To edit photos, tap the Edit button and use the controls in the toolbar to apply preset looks, adjust color and tone, fix red-eye, or crop and rotate the image. (See Chapter 4 for more detail on these types of tools, though I don't cover Revel specifically there.)

▶ **NOTE** In the spirit of sharing, Revel also enables you to upload a photo via Facebook, Twitter, Tumblr, or Flickr or to send it via email. Tap the Share button and choose an option.

Collaborate with Others

Here's where I find Revel the most interesting. From within Revel, you can share a library with someone else who has an Adobe ID, even if they don't subscribe to Revel. Here's how:

1. On your iPad, tap the hamburger icon (the three stacked horizontal lines; yes, that's the accepted generic term for that interface item) and then tap the Settings button to view your list of libraries in a popover.

2. Tap the Detail (>) button for the library you intend to share.

3. In the Sharing With section, tap the Add User button (8.16). (You can share a library with up to five people.)

4. Type the email address of the person who will share the library, and then tap Done.

5. Tap Done at the top of the popover to send an invitation.

8.16 Share the library with someone else.

When the other person installs the Revel software and signs in, they're asked if they want to join your library. After they do, the same rating and editing features are available. Images are updated nearly in real time, so when they mark a photo as a favorite, a gray flag indicates it's been marked by someone else (8.17). (The number in the flag tells you how many people have marked it.)

And because Revel also works on the Mac, when I get back to my computer, the files are already present in the desktop version of Revel. They reflect the ratings and edits made while reviewing.

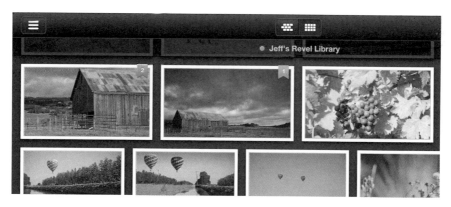

8.17 The other reviewer marked these two barn photos as favorites.

Print Photos from the iPad

When you think of printing from the iPad, you probably envision making a paper copy of an airline boarding pass or a text-only page of notes. Or, your first thought is, "The iPad can print?" The options for taking content from the iPad and putting it on paper are still relatively slim; a few Wi-Fi–enabled printers support Apple's AirPrint technology, for example. However, photos originated in the print world, and it is possible to transfer your images into ink-on-paper reproductions.

> ▶ **NOTE** Keep in mind that the iPad doesn't offer color management, so I wouldn't rely on it for professional output. Run your photos through a color-managed desktop workflow for the best results for clients, gallery shows, and the like.

Print from Nearly Any App

Since it's not possible to plug a printer into an iPad, any printing you do must occur wirelessly. If you own an AirPrint-compatible device, that's no problem: Tap the Share button in the Photos app, tap the Print button, and configure any printer-specific options.

If you own a perfectly good printer that doesn't support AirPrint, it's still possible to make it work. Using a utility called Printopia under OS X, any printer on the network that's accessible by your Mac is available (8.18). In fact, Printopia can also "print" to your Dropbox account, to folders on your computer, or directly to applications (8.19). Under Windows, check out Collobos Software's FingerPrint utility, which does the same thing.

The major printer manufacturers, like Epson, Lexmark, and HP, also offer free printing utilities for iOS that take advantage of their devices' features. (Make sure to check compatibility with your printer.)

8.18 Choose a printer and the number of copies, and hit Print.

8.19 Printopia prints to destinations other than printers.

Order Prints

A few companies are getting wise to the fact that some people use their iOS devices more than computers (or own just iPads), so they're developing apps that send images directly to print vendors. The app for the drugstore Walgreens, for example, lets you upload photos and then order prints or cards that you can pick up at the closest location.

Other fun apps include PopBooth, which takes photo booth–style snapshots and gives you the option of ordering a physical photo strip, and Sincerely's Ink Cards, which makes greeting cards from templates and your photos.

▶ **NOTE** If you're looking to order a print that's of higher quality than a snapshot from the iPad, a combination of an app and the Web might be the way to go. At the Web site Zenfolio (zenfolio.com), you can use the service Mpix.com to create and distribute prints. From my storefront (jeffcarlson.zenfolio.com), I can upload photos and then access the site in Safari to place an order.

Walgreens
for iPad

PopBooth

Ink Cards

https://it

https://it

Adobe Photoshop To

http://www.adobe.com

https://itunes.apple.c

iPhoto (Apple

http://www.ap

https://itune

App Reference

I knew there would be a lot of iPad apps mentioned in this book when I started, but I didn't want to pepper every paragraph with an app name, the price, and a lengthy link to the iTunes Store. Instead, this handy reference breaks down all the apps mentioned throughout each chapter, organized alphabetically, so you can find and investigate the apps easily. Where possible, I've included links to developers' Web sites, which often feature videos of the apps in action and more detail than what appears at the iTunes Store.

The iTunes Store links are regular Web addresses: Plug them into your favorite Web browser, which will redirect you to the product's page in iTunes. (Note that prices are current as of press time, but may change by the time you read this.)

Chapter 1: Capture Photos with the iPad

 AutoStitch Panorama for iPad (Cloudburst Research), $2.99

http://www.cloudburstresearch.com/

https://itunes.apple.com/us/app/autostitch-panorama-for-ipad/id586682453

 Blux Camera for iPad (Blux Touch), $2.99

http://bluxtouch.com/camera/

https://itunes.apple.com/us/app/blux-camera-for-ipad/id573827039

 Camera+ for iPad (tap tap tap), $0.99

http://campl.us/

http://itunes.apple.com/us/app/id550902799

 TrueHDR (Pictional LLC), $1.99

http://www.pictional.com/TrueHDR/

https://itunes.apple.com/us/app/true-hdr/id340741871

Chapter 2: The iPad on Location

 Box (Box, Inc.), Free

https://www.box.com/

https://itunes.apple.com/us/app/box-for-iphone-and-ipad/id290853822

 CameraMator (Wooblue), $24.99

http://www.cameramator.com/

https://itunes.apple.com/us/app/cameramator/id500195363

CamRanger (CamRanger), Free

http://www.camranger/

https://itunes.apple.com/us/app/camranger-wireless-dslr-camera/id552765874

Dropbox (Dropbox), Free

http://www.dropbox.com

http://itunes.apple.com/us/app/dropbox/id327630330

GarageBand (Apple), $4.99

http://www.apple.com/apps/garageband/

http://itunes.apple.com/us/app/garageband/id408709785

GeoSnitch (2ndNature), $1.99

http://www.shuttersnitch.com/geosnitch/

https://itunes.apple.com/us/app/geosnitch/id509857234

Geotag Photos Pro (TappyTaps), $3.99

http://www.geotagphotos.net/

http://itunes.apple.com/us/app/geotag-photos-pro/id355503746

iMovie for iOS (Apple), $4.99

http://www.apple.com/ipad/from-the-app-store/apps-by-apple/imovie.html

http://itunes.apple.com/us/app/imovie/id377298193

PhotoSync (touchbyte GmbH), $1.99

http://www.photosync-app.com/

http://itunes.apple.com/us/app/photosync-wirelessly-transfers/id415850124

PlainText (Hog Bay Software), Free

http://www.hogbaysoftware.com/products/plaintext

http://itunes.apple.com/us/app/plaintext-dropbox-text-editing/id391254385

Seagate Media (Seagate Technology), Free

http://www.seagate.com/external-hard-drives/

https://itunes.apple.com/us/app/seagate-media/id431912202

ShutterSnitch (2ndNature), $19.99

http://www.shuttersnitch.com/

http://itunes.apple.com/us/app/shuttersnitch/id364176211

Skype for iPad (Skype), Free

http://www.skype.com/

http://itunes.apple.com/us/app/skype-for-ipad/id442012681

SoftBox Pro for iPad (EggErr Studio), $2.99

http://itunes.apple.com/us/app/softbox-pro-for-ipad/id415056105

SugarSync (SugarSync), Free

http://www.sugarsync.com

http://itunes.apple.com/us/app/sugarsync/id288491637

Chapter 3: The iPad in the Studio

Adobe Nav for Photoshop (Adobe), $1.99

http://www.photoshop.com/products/mobile/nav

http://itunes.apple.com/us/app/adobe-nav-for-photoshop/id426614130

Air Display (Avatron Software), $9.99

http://avatron.com/apps

http://itunes.apple.com/us/app/air-display/id368158927

Blux Camera for iPad (Blux touch), $0.99

http://bluxtouch.com/camera/

https://itunes.apple.com/us/app/blux-camera-for-ipad/id573827039

Blux Lens (Blux Touch), $0.99

http://bluxtouch.com/camera/lens.html

https://itunes.apple.com/us/app/blux-lens/id598230244

CameraMator (Wooblue), $24.99

http://www.cameramator.com/

https://itunes.apple.com/us/app/cameramator/id500195363

CamNexus (Wooblue), Free*

http://www.camnexus.com/

The app was not yet available at press time.

CamRanger (CamRanger), Free

http://www.camranger/

https://itunes.apple.com/us/app/camranger-wireless-dslr-camera/id552765874

Capture Pilot (Phase One), Free*

http://www.phaseone.com/capturepilot

http://itunes.apple.com/us/app/capture-pilot/id404906435

Capture Pilot requires Phase One's $299 Capture One Pro software.

iUSBportCamera (Sanho), Free*

http://www.hypershop.com/HyperDrive-iUSBportCAMERA-p/iusb-cam.htm

The app was not yet available at press time.

iStopMotion for iPad (Boinx Software), $9.99

http://boinx.com/istopmotion/ipad/

http://itunes.apple.com/us/app/istopmotion-for-ipad/id484019696

iStopMotion Remote Camera (Boinx Software), Free

http://boinx.com/istopmotion/ipad/

http://itunes.apple.com/us/app/istopmotion-remote-camera/id484024876

Triggertrap (Triggertrap), Free

http://www.triggertrap.com/

https://itunes.apple.com/us/app/triggertrap/id517679831

Chapter 4: Rate and Tag Photos

Photogene for iPad (Mobile Pond), $2.99

http://www.mobile-pond.com/mobile-pond/products.html

http://itunes.apple.com/us/app/photogene-for-ipad/id363448251

Photosmith (C² Enterprises), $19.99

http://www.photosmithapp.com/

http://itunes.apple.com/us/app/photosmith/id427757668

PhotosInfoPro (Dmitri Toropov), $4.99

http://www.photosinfopro.com/

https://itunes.apple.com/app/photosinfo-pro/id435368159

Chapter 5: Edit Photos on the iPad

Adobe Photoshop Touch (Adobe), $9.99

http://www.adobe.com/products/photoshop-touch.html

https://itunes.apple.com/us/app/adobe-photoshop-touch/id495716481

iPhoto (Apple), $4.99

http://www.apple.com/apps/iphoto/

https://itunes.apple.com/us/app/iphoto/id497786065

Photogene for iPad (Mobile Pond), $2.99

http://www.mobile-pond.com/mobile-pond/products.html

http://itunes.apple.com/us/app/photogene-for-ipad/id363448251

PhotoRaw (Alexander McGuffog), $9.99

http://sites.google.com/site/iphotoraw/

http://itunes.apple.com/us/app/photoraw/id413899112

PhotoRaw Lite (Alexander McGuffog), Free

http://sites.google.com/site/iphotoraw/

https://itunes.apple.com/us/app/photoraw-lite/id423201178

piRAWnha (Cypress Innovations), $9.99

http://pirawnha.com/

http://itunes.apple.com/us/app/pirawnha/id409747795

Snapseed (Nik Software), Free

http://www.snapseed.com/

http://itunes.apple.com/us/app/snapseed/id439438619

Handy Photo (Adva Soft), $1.99

http://adva-soft.com/products/handy-photo/

https://itunes.apple.com/app/handy-photo/id598565205

Chapter 6: Edit Video on the iPad

iMovie for iOS (Apple), $4.99

http://www.apple.com/ipad/from-the-app-store/apps-by-apple/imovie.html

http://itunes.apple.com/us/app/imovie/id377298193

Pinnacle Studio (Corel), $12.99

http://www.pinnaclesys.com/

https://itunes.apple.com/us/app/pinnacle-studio/id552100086

Chapter 7: Build an iPad Portfolio

Portfolio for iPad (Britton Mobile Development), $12.99

http://ipadportfolioapp.com/

http://itunes.apple.com/us/app/portfolio-for-ipad/id384210950

Chapter 8: Share Photos

500px (500px), Free

http://500px.com/ipad

http://itunes.apple.com/us/app/500px/id471965292

Adobe Revel (Adobe), Free*

http://www.adobe.com/go/revel_learnmore

http://itunes.apple.com/us/app/adobe-revel/id455066445

* $5.99 monthly subscription required after demo period.

Camera Awesome (SmugMug), Free

http://www.awesomize.com/

https://itunes.apple.com/us/app/camera-awesome/id420744028?mt=8

Flickr (Yahoo!), Free

http://mobile.yahoo.com/flickr/iphone

http://itunes.apple.com/us/app/flickr/id328407587

FlickStackr for Flickr (iPont), $1.99

http://ipont.ca/ip/flickstackr/

https://itunes.apple.com/us/app/flickstackr-for-flickr/id364895358

Ink Cards (Sincerely, Inc.), Free

http://www.sincerely.com/ink

http://itunes.apple.com/us/app/sincerely-ink-cards-create/id477296657

Photogene for iPad (Mobile Pond), $2.99

http://www.mobile-pond.com/mobile-pond/products.html

http://itunes.apple.com/us/app/photogene-for-ipad/id363448251

PhotoStackr for 500px (iPont), $0.99

http://ipont.ca/

http://itunes.apple.com/us/app/photostackr-for-500px/id468659684

PopBooth (Sincerely, Inc.), Free

http://popbooth.com/

http://itunes.apple.com/us/app/popbooth-photo-booth/id432092216

SmugMug (SmugMug), Free

http://www.smugmug.com/ipad

http://itunes.apple.com/us/app/smugmug/id364894061

Walgreens for iPad (Walgreen Co.), Free

http://www.walgreens.com

https://itunes.apple.com/us/app/walgreens-for-ipad/id430444027

INDEX

shooting photos
    with Camera app, 4–5
    with Camera+ for iPad, 6–7
    timer, 7
shooting video, 4
shutter button, 4
ShutterSnitch app, 28–29, 33, 200
Sincerely Ink Cards app, 195, 205
skin tones, 116
Skype for iPad app, 26, 200
slideshows, 156, 165, 174. *See also*
    portfolios
Smart Group feature, 74–75
SmugMug app, 186, 204
SmugShot app, 186
Snapseed app
    brightness adjustment, 102
    contrast adjustment, 102
    cropping photos, 99
    image editing in, 98–103
    obtaining, 203
    recomposing photos, 99–100
    straightening photos, 100
    uploading photos from, 180–181
SoftBox Pro app, 42, 200
sorting photos, 73
sound. *See* audio
sound effects, 118, 146, 149
special effects. *See* effects
splitting clips, 138
stabilization, image, 6
stands, 55–57
star ratings. *See* rating photos
stop-motion video, 58–60
straightening photos
    in iPhoto, 112–113
    in Photogene, 104–105
    in Photos app, 97
    in Photoshop Touch, 120
    in Snapseed, 100
studio, using iPad in, 45–60
The Stump, 56–57
SugarSync app, 38, 200

T

tagging. *See* keywords
terminology, xvii
Tether Tools, 55–56
tethered cameras, 46, 55–56
theme music, 147
themes, movies, 133
thumbnails, 112, 171, 175
time-lapse shots, 52–54
time-lapse video, 60
timeline, iMovie, 132, 134–139, 150
timer, 7, 52, 54, 60
tone
    adjusting, 96
    adjusting in iPhoto, 114, 117
    adjusting in Photogene, 105–109
    adjusting in Photoshop Touch, 122
    adjusting in Snapseed, 100–103
Toshiba wireless memory cards, 27
Transcend wireless memory cards, 27
transitions, video, 138, 139, 140
Triggertrap app, 53–54, 202
trimming clips, 137
TrueHDR app, 8, 198
Tumblr, 192
TVs
    wired connections to, 174–176
    wireless connections to, 177
Twitter, 180–183, 192

U

uploading photos. *See also* sharing
    photos
    Camera Awesome, 186
    Dropbox, 35
    to from editing apps, 180–183
    Flickr, 185
    iCloud Photo Stream, 35, 36–37,
      184
    to photo sharing services, 180–183
    from Photogene, 181–183
    PhotoStackr for 500px, 186
    from Snapseed, 180–181
    via photo service apps, 185–186